AMY ALLEN
CREATIVE CO.

PHOTOGRAPHER & PROFESSIONAL THIRD WHEELER

WWW.AACREATIVECO.COM @AMYALLENCREATIVECO DUBBO & AUSTRALIA WIDE

DANCING WITH THEM

CELEBRATING LGBTQ+ PEOPLE IN LOVE

MAGAZINE | BLOG | DIRECTORY

www.dancingwiththem.com

EDITOR & CO-FOUNDER
Tara Baker

PARTNERSHIPS & CO-FOUNDER
Arlia Hassell

CONTRIBUTING PHOTOGRAPHERS
Fox & Kin, Kira McGrigg Photo, Jennifer Moher, Dewitt for Love, Mari Sabra Photography, Jennifer See Studios, Sarah McClure Photo, AmorVincitOmnia, Shane Shepherd, Jacqie Q Photography, Lorena Leon, Fox & Twig, Silk & Thorn, Kristyn Taulane Photography, Dani Knight & Co, Phan Tien Photography

BACK COVER IMAGE
Fox & Kin
www.foxandkin.com

SUBMISSIONS
www.dancingwithher.com/submissions

ADVERTISING & WHOLESALE ENQUIRIES
partnerships@dancingwithher.com

DANCING WITH HER
Dja Dja Wurrung
Bendigo, Victoria, Australia

JOIN OUR COMMUNITY
www.dancingwithher.com

facebook.com/dancingwithher
instagram.com/dancingwithher
pinterest.com/dancingwithher

Dancing With Her acknowledges the Australian Aboriginal and Torres Strait Islander peoples of this nation. We acknowledge the Dja Dja Wurrung people whose Land on which our company is located and where we primarily conduct our business. We pay our respects to Ancestors and Elders, past, present and emerging. Dancing With Her is committed to honoring Australian Aboriginal and Torres Strait Islander Peoples unique cultural and spiritual relationships to the land, waters and seas and their rich contribution to society.

© 2021 Dancing With Her®
All rights reserved. Reproduction in whole or part without permission is strictly prohibited.

010
THINGS WE LOVE

012
GABY & KATE

018
ADRIANNA & LYDIA

025
HOW TO CREATE A MEANINGFUL WEDDING CEREMONY

026
MARIE & OISIN

034
ALEX & DELANEY

039
A TEN YEAR LOVE STORY

042
A CELESTIAL INSPIRED INTIMATE AFFAIR

046
ALICIA & PAVITHRA

054
ANGIE & LAURA

061
UNPLUGGED WEDDINGS

062
CAITLIN & FRANCES

068
JUSTINE & SARAH

076
MAR & XIOMARA

081
HOW TO CHOOSE YOUR WEDDING VENDORS

082
FRANCES & JESSIE

088
A GUIDE TO WEDDING WEBSITES

090
CHARLENE & MARKIA

094
HOW TO HIRE ELOPEMENT WEDDING VENDORS

098
BOHO GLAM

102
LAUREN & TEEGAN

108
WHY YOU SHOULDN'T NEGOTIATE WITH YOUR WEDDING VENDORS

110
A LUXE TROPICAL BOHO AFFAIR

119
THE LIST

HELLO

When we started our magazine four years ago, almost to the date, we never imagined we'd find ourselves sitting here introducing our tenth edition.

Welcome, to Volume Ten of Dancing With Her Magazine.

Pinch us.

This issue celebrates the couples who have married around restrictions of a pandemic. Some have downsized their guest list, others chose to elope. One couple, Lauren and Teegan, had only one guest- their dog, Blue.

Inside these pages you'll read about couples who have epic love stories; Oisin and Marie in particular had such a unique way of getting to know each other. We get the opportunity to share Alicia and Pavithra's love story, one that triumphs conservative Mormon and Hindu backgrounds. And, Caitlin and Frances, who, after twenty years together, have decided to tie the knot legally.

Inside are stories from across the world; the US, Australia, Italy, Spain and Vietnam- they all have one thing in common. At the core of them all, they celebrate incredible love. We know that you'll find inspiration not just for your own wedding day between these pages, but they'll also inspire your relationships.

Whether this is the very first issue you've held, or read online, or it is your tenth - thank you. Thank you for being here, for supporting our work and for helping us to continue to inspire other couples whose relationships look so similar to yours.

Our cups are filled. We are so grateful.

Now, to celebrate. Cheers to another ten more issues of this magazine- a magazine that celebrates love.

All our love,
Arlia & Tara

Emily Howlett
PHOTOGRAPHY

fun . natural . relaxed

emilyhowlettphotography@live.com.au

www.howlettphotographyweddings.com

@emilyhowlettphotography

FOUR STYLISTS YOU NEED TO FOLLOW ON INSTAGRAM FOR ULTIMATE HANGING INSTALLATION INSPIRATION

01
@banginhangins

Hello zero-waste installs that pack a whole lotta personality! When it comes to creativity, Bangin Hangins knocks it right out of the park - their installs are just so much fun!

02
@streamadelica_uk

Yep, those beauties hanging from the ceiling are completely weatherproof and, the best part, totally reusable. Hello, Eco-friendly. Time to add a little sparkle to your styling.

03
@epic_installs_

While Epic Installs do bring to life some awesome hanging installations, they also happen to create some epic streamer walls too - which can pack just as much punch.

04
@thecolorcondition

So much color, so much sparkle, The Color Condition really do have a huge selection of different hangings to suit any type of wedding vibe you might be trying to achieve.

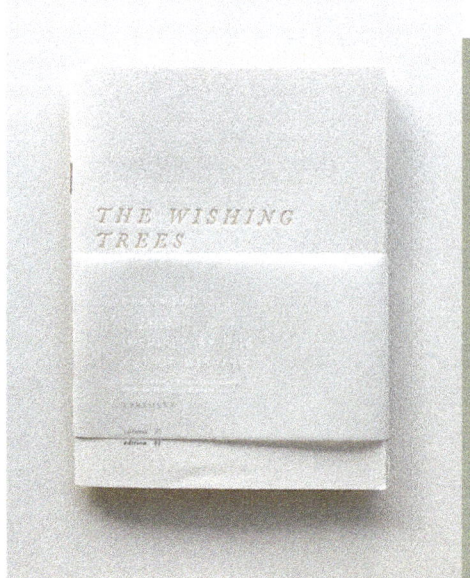

If you've been searching for the perfect gift for someone who really does have it all, these stunning letterpress zines, full of quotes, are the perfect choice.

We adore the Wishing Trees edition - a zine that is full of quotes inspired by the act of wishing. There's also one inspired by the sun and moon that is just so beautiful.

And, for the real romantics, they're released bi-monthly, which means you can woo your lover just because a little more often.

Ah, we'll be keeping these safe and enjoying them for years to come.

www.thelittlepress.net

If you're a human who menstruates, and you haven't already jumped on the period underwear bandwagon, allow us to introduce these Bloody Comfy Period Undies by Bonds.

Not only are they comfy, these reusable undies replace the need for single-use pads, tampons and liners- so much kinder to the environment! So long as you rinse and wash according to the label, one pair will last just as long as any other pair of Bonds underwear - which in our experience is quite a while. Just think of all the landfill rubbish you'll be saving!

The best part is that they are really comfy - Bloody Comfy Period Undies is a name that is well deserved.

www.bonds.com.au

Could you imagine sitting in your home, next to your lover, creating your very own unique jewelry? No, we couldn't either until now.

CAST have helped hundreds of couples ditch mass-produced, cliche wedding rings in favour of bespoke modern heirlooms, steeped in ancient tradition and made with feeling. And by feeling, we mean you'll do it yourself.

They send out these handy kits that have all the tools and information on how to create your very own one-of-a-kind piece.

It's a whole lot of fun, and a whole lot of memory making.

www.experiencecast.com

Okay, we think we might have just found the perfect gift for your wedding party - premium Turkish linen by Købn.

Sustainability and transparency is at the core of Købn, which means that these towels don't just feel luxurious, they are also good for the earth. They're also made with traceable materials in safe and socially responsible workplaces and environmentally friendly facilities - every product even comes with a QR code to access full traceability of the fibers and the farms used to bring it to life.

They're as good as they sound, promise.

www.kobn.com.au

Have you ever heard of a skincare brand that works directly with farmers to press oils and grow herns specifically for their products?

No, neither. And, that's because it's mostly unheard of in the skincare industry.

Avec's products are as fresh as you can get, really. And, they work. We particularly love the Bio-active Nutrient Serum - it feels so incredibly light on your skin and leaves your skin smelling rather delicious.

Also, Avec is women-owned and a portion of every purchase goes towards women experiencing family violence. So, good for your skin and making a difference in the world.

www.avecskin.com

Way back in 2013, State of Escape released a neoprene bag - and they kind've swept the world.

These lightweight, handcrafted bags are the perfect bag to throw everything you need on the wedding day into. We're in love with their new cactus color - a perfect go-with-everything color that isn't just your boring black.

And, because your bag shouldn't just be good for your wedding day, these ones come with a lifetime warranty. You'll be carrying it around for quite a lot longer than your wedding day hangover.

www.stateofescape.com

Do you want to grab a copy of our print magazine, to have and to hold? With free global shipping, each issue is filled with incredible wedding inspiration.

www.dancingwithher.com/magazine

GABY & KATE
PHOTOGRAPHY BY FOX AND KIN
www.foxandkin.com

MELBOURNE, AUSTRALIA

Gaby and Kate met five and a half years ago. Kate was traveling around South East Asia by herself. Gaby had booked a trip around Cambodia and Vietnam with one of her friends; however, the Vietnamese embassy lost her friend's passport- so Gaby too ended up traveling alone. They were both booked on a tour around Cambodia. It started on Christmas Day, and to be more financially viable, the tour group made them roommates. And that's where our romance began.

After a whirlwind eight days, Gaby went back home to Australia and Kate kept on traveling.

It was only when Kate went back to Sydney and was stranded a night, due to car troubles en route back to Port Macquarie that she decided to catch up for coffee with Gaby. They agreed that it wasn't just a holiday fling and maybe they could fit into each other's lives. So after getting to know each other a bit more, they did two years of long-distance while Kate finished her degree.

Gaby proposed to Kate just before Christmas. Kate's always been the 'organized one,' the 'impossible to surprise one.' But when Gaby suggested they open some Christmas presents early, Kate predictably obliged. Gaby was acting weird, Kate didn't know why because she knew she had gotten her an Apple Watch. When Gaby finally gave Kate her 'Apple Watch,' she opened the box and inside there was a ring and letter. For Kate, knowing Gaby was as confident as she was that they would spend the rest of their lives together was pretty damn cool.

Gaby and Kate eloped, at first. They shared vows next to a bonfire during an intimate ceremony at night. However, they'd always spoken of the priorities of marriage being not just a commitment to one another, but wanting to also throw a big party with their family and friends. It was really important to the couple that they take a moment to thank them for all of their love and support towards them as a couple. Even with the delays in wedding planning and rescheduling due to lock downs, that priority never waivered.

They fell in love with their venue, Rupert on Rupert from the beginning. The 'bringing the outdoors in' vibe was perfect, but they'd also seen how they could throw together an epic feast and serve up incredible cocktails. They flew their DJ, Charlie Villas, in from Sydney after watching her spark up the dance floor at queer parties across Sydney and giant clusters of disco balls were a must in terms of styling. They opted out when it came to florals; the greenery of the venue coupled with candles and their DIY menus was enough. And, they couldn't think of a better human to capture every moment of the celebration than Nic, of Fox and Kin, whose work they'd admired from afar for quite some time.

The wedding day started with the brides getting their hair and makeup done. They then wandered through the streets of Collingwood for their couples portraits before arriving at their venue where they were met with their guests already enjoying the cocktails.

They had a good friend MC, who introduced them to the party, before canapes and more drinks flowed. They had an incredible seated candlelit feast, with the fireplace roaring- it was a rainy day so it made the vibe of the room even more incredible.

The speeches had always been one of their favorite parts of the wedding day, and their speeches were no exception of this. Dessert was a cannoli cart and espresso martinis, then the party really got started on the disco ball dance floor.

For Gaby and Kate, they've learned together over the past few years that the future is entirely unpredictable, and so any opportunity that affords itself is worth taking (or at least considering). They aren't sure what the future holds, but know just how lovely it is to have one another.

Catering & Venue Rupert on Rupert | **Entertainment** DJ Charlie Villas | **Gown Designers** One Day Bridal/KYHA Studios, MLM Label | **H&MU** The Distinctive Dame | **Photographer** Fox & Kin | **Robes** Bed Threads | **Transport** Uber

ADRIANNA & LYDIA
PHOTOGRAPHY BY KIRA MCGRIGG PHOTO
www.kiramcgriggphoto.com

UTAH, UNITED STATES OF AMERICA

Some of the greatest love stories start as friendships. And, that's how Adrianna and Lydia's story begins. First meeting at high school seven years ago, they didn't take things beyond a friendship level for four years.

The first night they spent together was something unforgettable. They sat together, crying tears of joy. They both knew that it was the start of something incredible.

Their proposal was intimate and personal.

Lydia proposed first. Ordering an engagement ring from Do Amore and it arrived just in time for a Valentine's Day date she'd planned. Sitting on the couch before they left, Lydia got down on one knee in their living room. It was everything Adrianna had always dreamt of.

The idea of an elopement always intrigued Adrianna and Lydia. It meant they could have something intimate and private while saving money. They also were attracted to the thought of wedding planning that was worry-free.

Being able to take a small group of friends to a beautiful location and get married was an opportunity far too good to pass up. And, with the love of outdoors, they couldn't think of a location any more perfect than Northern Michigan.

They invited four of their best friends and rented a cabin overlooking Lake Superior. The night before the wedding was filled with celebratory cocktails and laughter - opening gifts from the nearly-weds closest family and friends.

It was an early and cold start on the wedding morning. At 3:30am they woke to arrive at Black Rocks State Park in Marquette, Michigan before sunrise. Adrianna got ready upstairs, Lydia downstairs. It was important to them both that they didn't see one another prior to the ceremony so instead, they gave each other a handwritten note to read while they were getting ready.

It was a twenty-minute drive to the ceremony location from the cabin. Lydia arrived first with friends to set up the location, Adrianna arriving shortly after.

After a quick first look, they moved straight into the ceremony. Officiated by their best friend, Jenna, it was emotional and personal - not a dry eye in sight.

As the ceremony concluded, they popped champagne and cozied up in a blanket. The day was filled with couples photos, capturing memories of the day that seemed to be flying by.

As the day ended, Adrianna and Lydia rented a private room at local restaurant, The Delft Bistro. The converted old movie theatre was now a dining establishment and a perfect choice for the two movie-loving newlyweds. They wined and dined celebrating their new union as married.

And, now that they're married, Adrianna and Lydia are dreaming of honeymooning out west with their Suburu Crosstrek, camping their way through the national parks for a few weeks making memories together that will last a lifetime.

Cake Walmart | **Cake Topper & Florist** Ling's Moment | **Ceremony Venue** Presque Isle Black Rocks State Park | **Decorative Elements** Target, KayleighDuMond | **Dress & Shoes** ASOS | **Earrings** Monica Vinader | **Engagement & Wedding Rings** Do Amore | **Jumpsuit** Lulus | **Officiant** Jenna Faber | **Photographer** Kira McGrigg Photography | **Reception Venue** The Delft Bistro | **Stationery** KayleighDuMond | **Suit** J Crew

Photography by Sylviane Brauer

HOW TO CREATE A MEANINGFUL WEDDING CEREMONY
Contributed by Celebrant Kate
www.celebrantkate.com.au

Whether you're having two guests or two hundred, having a meaningful ceremony is the difference between it feeling like a formality or being your absolute favorite part of the day!

If you're reading this I probably don't need to tell you that the decision to get married is a big deal, you're choosing to spend the rest of your life with someone! The moment where you commit to that, your ceremony, is so profound. You don't arrive at that moment without a story, a journey to this point, and this is your one opportunity to mark a moment in time in whatever way feels right for you.

Often when people think about wedding ceremonies there's a lot of subconscious expectations and preconceived ideas of what a ceremony looks like. Wedding ceremonies often go hand-in-hand with a bunch of 'shoulds.' I'm often asked questions that start with 'should I...' For example, should I walk down the aisle on the left or right? My response is to always explore what feels right to you, because what feels right for you is exactly what you should be doing, and that might not be walking down an aisle at all, it might be starting your ceremony with you already up the front, holding hands, together.

Anything that someone else tells you to do, or that gets included without thinking about what it means to you, will feel more like a formality and a bit disconnected for both you and your guests. For your guests it feels as if they're watching something happen rather than being part of something really special.

Every single one of us has a story and there is amazing beauty in all the things that make each and every one of us different. Creating your ceremony so that it's authentic to you gives it true meaning. It will feel amazing on the day, your guests will feel like they've experienced something really special, and it will be a moment in time you'll never forget!

So how do you create a ceremony with meaning?

First, give yourself a blank canvas to create from. In most parts of the world there are just a handful of things that have to be part of your ceremony to make it legal. Usually these entail the celebrant or officiant stating your full legal names, saying legal vows and signing legal documents. It's best to ask your celebrant or officiant.

Everything else in your ceremony is completely your choice! This is your blank canvas!

Ask yourself some questions to explore your meaning...

- What does getting married mean to you both?
- What does it mean to gather in the spot you've chosen?
- What does it mean to you to have the two or two hundred friends and family with you in this moment?

Saying some words in your ceremony about your relationship connects you and your guests to what you're celebrating - you! It can be just a couple of lines expressing the essence of your relationship, maybe some stories from your time together, or anything else that feels right to you.

Here's some questions to start exploring what's meaningful to you about your relationship...

- What attracted you to each other?
- How did life change after you met?
- What do you value most about the relationship you've created?
- How do you help each other be the best you can be?
- What have you achieved together and how did your relationship make that happen?

These questions are just a starting point. Some people find it really hard to answer them, for others the answers come flowing out. Finding a celebrant that is willing to explore your meaning, help you find your story and generate ideas to celebrate you in a way that feels right to you is super important.

Getting married during a pandemic has shown me just how important a ceremony that celebrates you really is. As couples have adapted to public health restrictions, rescheduled dates, changed venues, reduced guest lists and the million other things that they've navigated with getting married in a pandemic, the one thing that hasn't changed is their love for each other. Throughout the pandemic I've been working with couples to write their ceremony even when we're unsure about when or where it will be. Writing down your meaning, or your story, can help remind you of the wonderfulness of your relationship (that doesn't change) and connect you to what you're truly celebrating, whenever the day comes and whatever it ends up looking like.

MARIE & OISIN

PHOTOGRAPHY BY JENNIFER MOHER
www.jennifermoher.com

TORONTO, CANADA

Their love story started long distance. Between Windsor and Toronto, they experienced the most crushing heart sickness. But, it wasn't all incredibly difficult. The first few months put pressure on them to make the most of every moment together. They built blanket forts, went for sky walks through the forest, tried different restaurants and cafes every weekend, and surprised one another with surprise gifts and unplanned visits.

Winding back, before they had said 'I love you', or held hands, or even kissed, Marie and Oisin planned a listening party. The goal was simple; solidify their friendship.

The rules were simple. Make a playlist of every single important song from your childhood right through to the present day and then you had only the duration of the song to explain to the person its importance to your life, your journey, your story, your history - an expedited exploration of each other's lives through music.

They each made long playlists. Hours of music. In the early evening, they each set up their playlists on their respective devices and hit shuffle. Over the next hours, into the wee hours of the next morning, they fell in love. They cried and laughed. They told stories of their first kiss, their first loves, first heartbreaks. They introduced songs to each other that their grandparents had first shared with them and reminisced over the songs that they first learned on guitar.

There were months of long-distance romancing. For a while, Oisin considered leaving Toronto but after one particularly surreal date, at the Fergus Scottish Festival, Marie reached over, took Oisin's hand, and said, 'Don't come back, I'm coming to you.' Oisin still cries, filling with relief and love, when they reflect back on the moment.

Marie found a ring in a secondhand store the week before they were supposed to go back to Windsor with Oisin for the first time. They'd talked about being married often but without any urgency so finding the perfect ring felt like a sign. While sitting outside the bar where they had shared their first date, once again talking about the hypotheticals of getting married, Marie pulled out a vintage brass pillbox containing the ring, placed it on Oisin's knee, and said, 'Will you really marry me? Really really?'.

The moment was perfect, without any planning.

Their wedding was tiny and, much like their engagement, perfect.

En route to the venue, they chose to have their newlywed portraits at the subway station because for them it's a place that has meaning. Each day on their commute to work they text one another '...last outside bit. I love you!' Before heading underground and losing service.

Their wedding was in a bar, in the evening. Friends spoke, but there wasn't a wedding party. The dress code was 'whatever makes you feel a million bucks' and vows were short and sweet. The newlyweds made some of the desserts themselves, others were locally catered. The Trinidadian street food was catered by a friend, and friends were serving from behind the bar. There wasn't anyone there that they didn't know, or who wasn't invested in their love.

100%, the entire day was their wedding, their terms. There was nothing that Marie or Oisin compromised on. They wore what they wanted, ate what they wanted, and invited whom they wanted.

For Marie and Oisin, 'All in. All ways. Always.'

FAMILY FRUIT AND FLOWER
COCKTAILS
PONY BOY
SPRING
COCKTAILS
PONY BOY
SPRING CLEAN
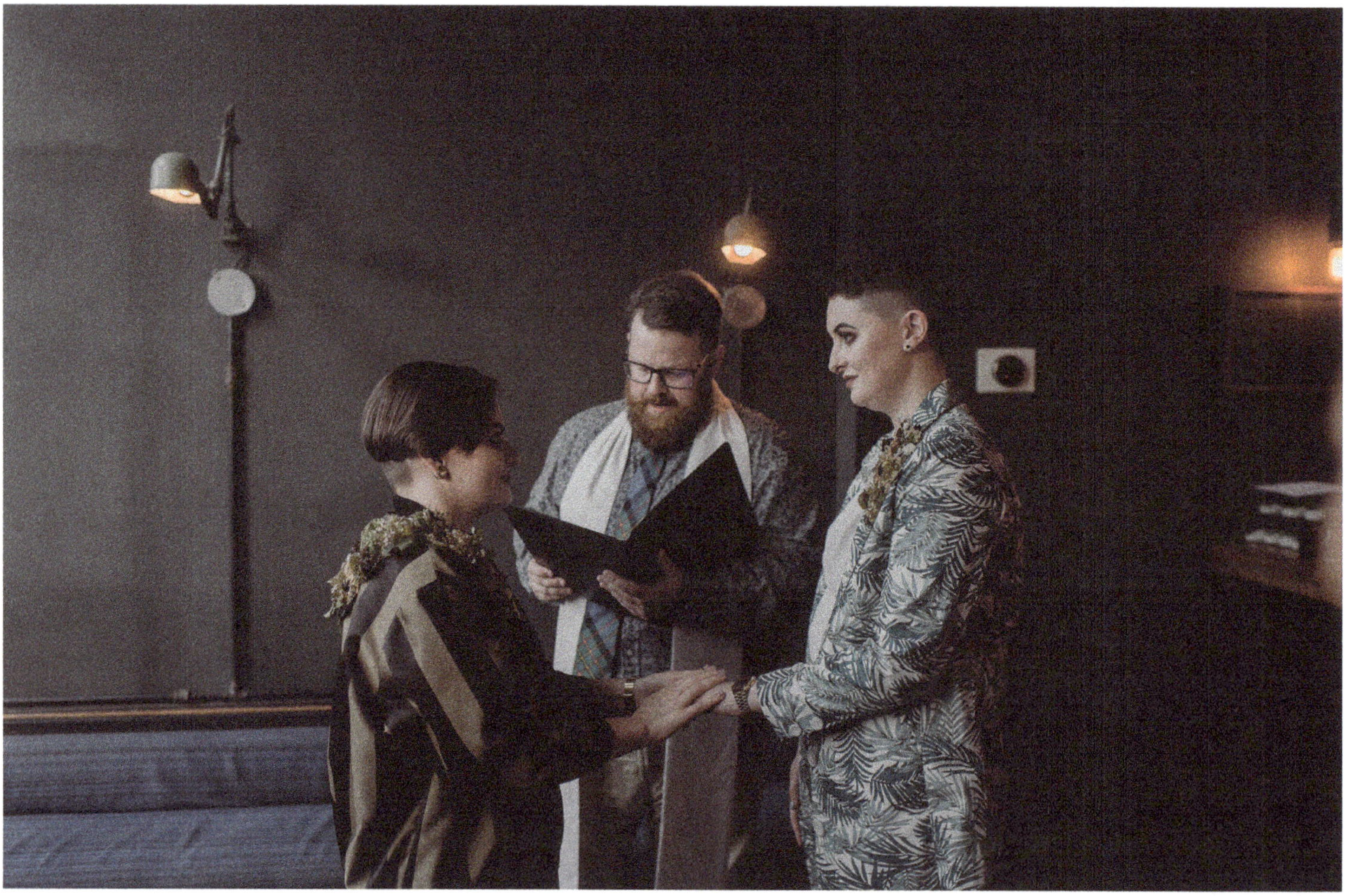

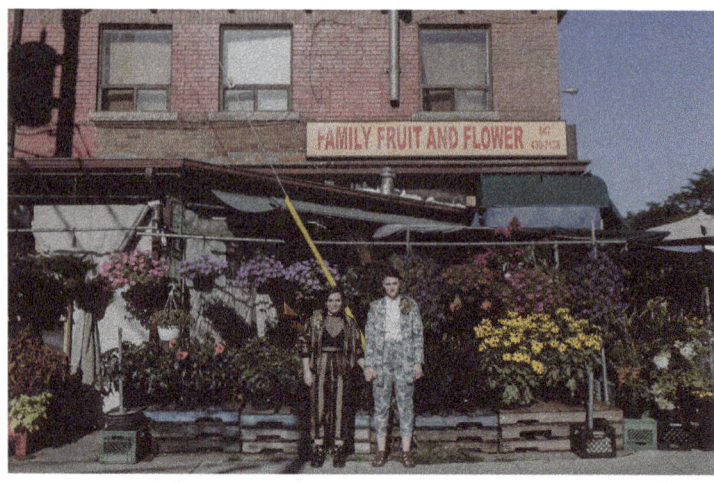

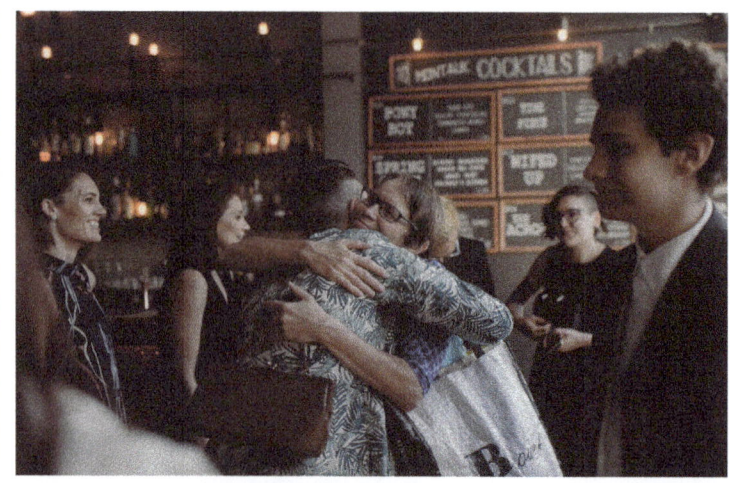

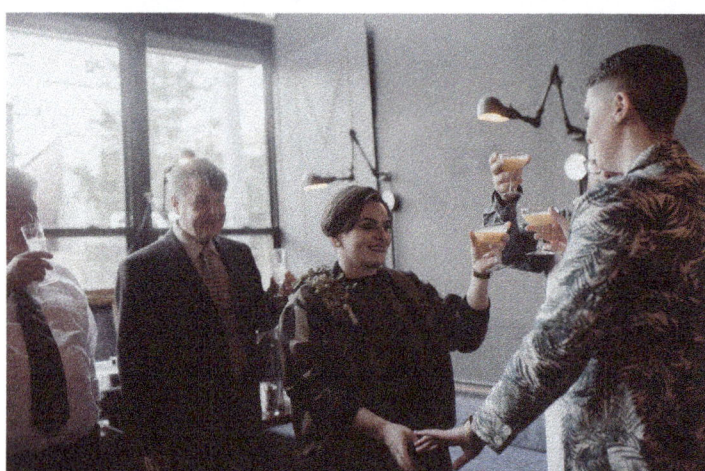

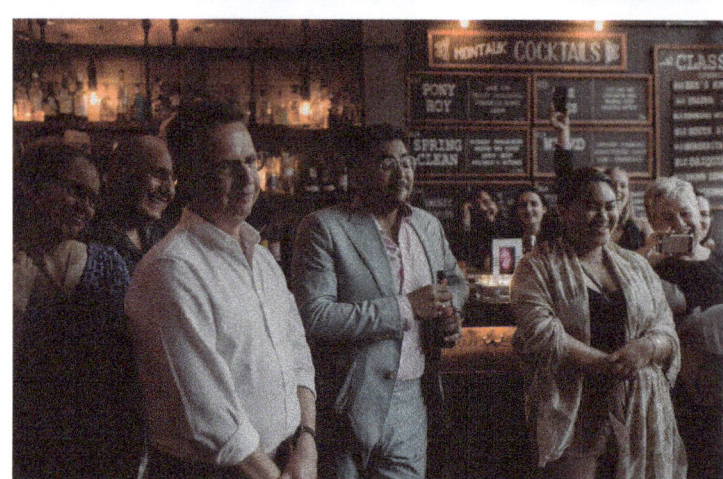

Catering Young Animal Catering | **Celebrant** Reilly McLaren | **Desserts** Eve's Temptations, St. Lawrence Market | **Favors** Moss Ball Pets | **Flowers** Harris Flower Farm | **Makeup** Ciera Jewel | **Photographer** Jennifer Moher | **Rings** William's Jewellers | **Suits** House Of Glass, Wildfang

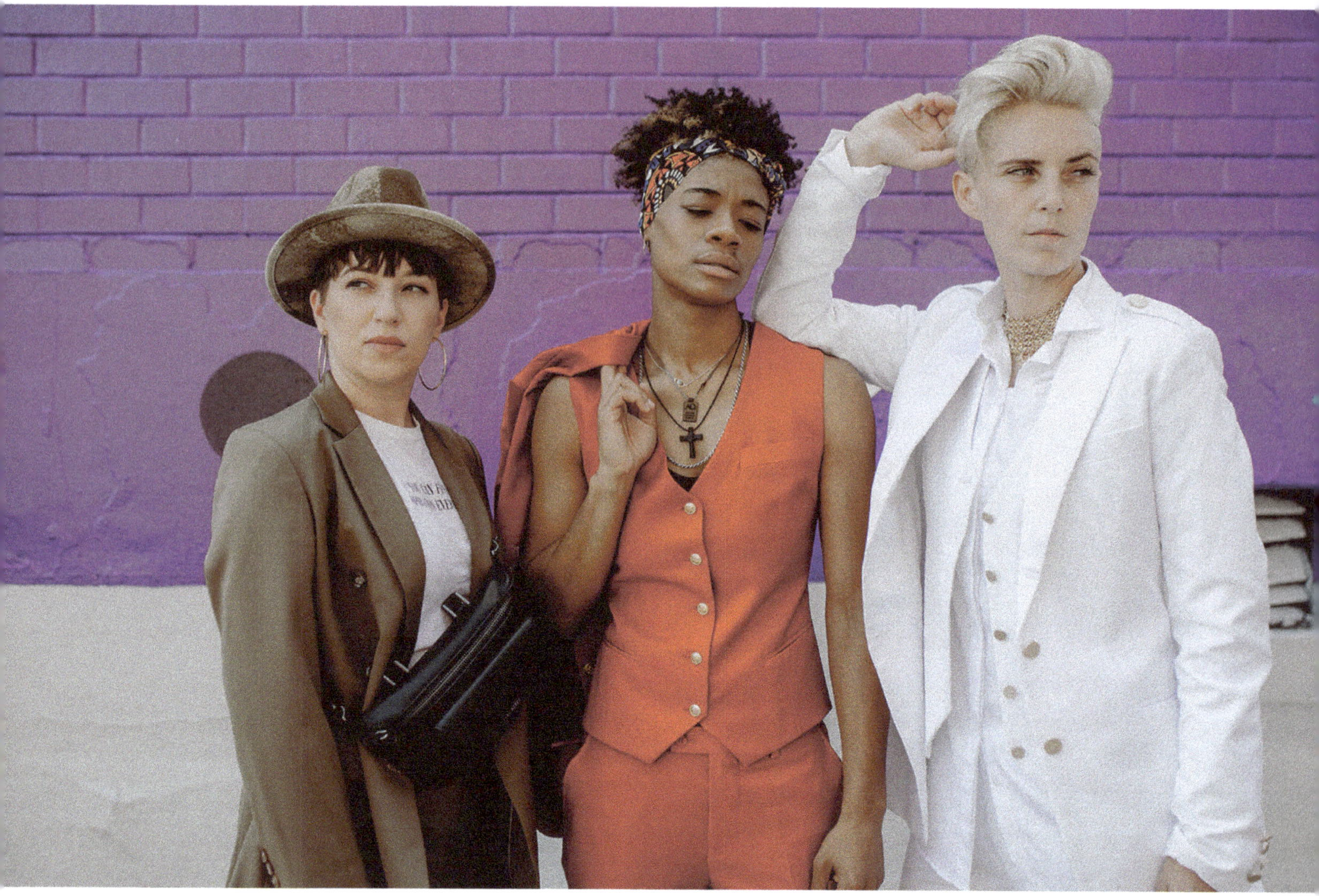

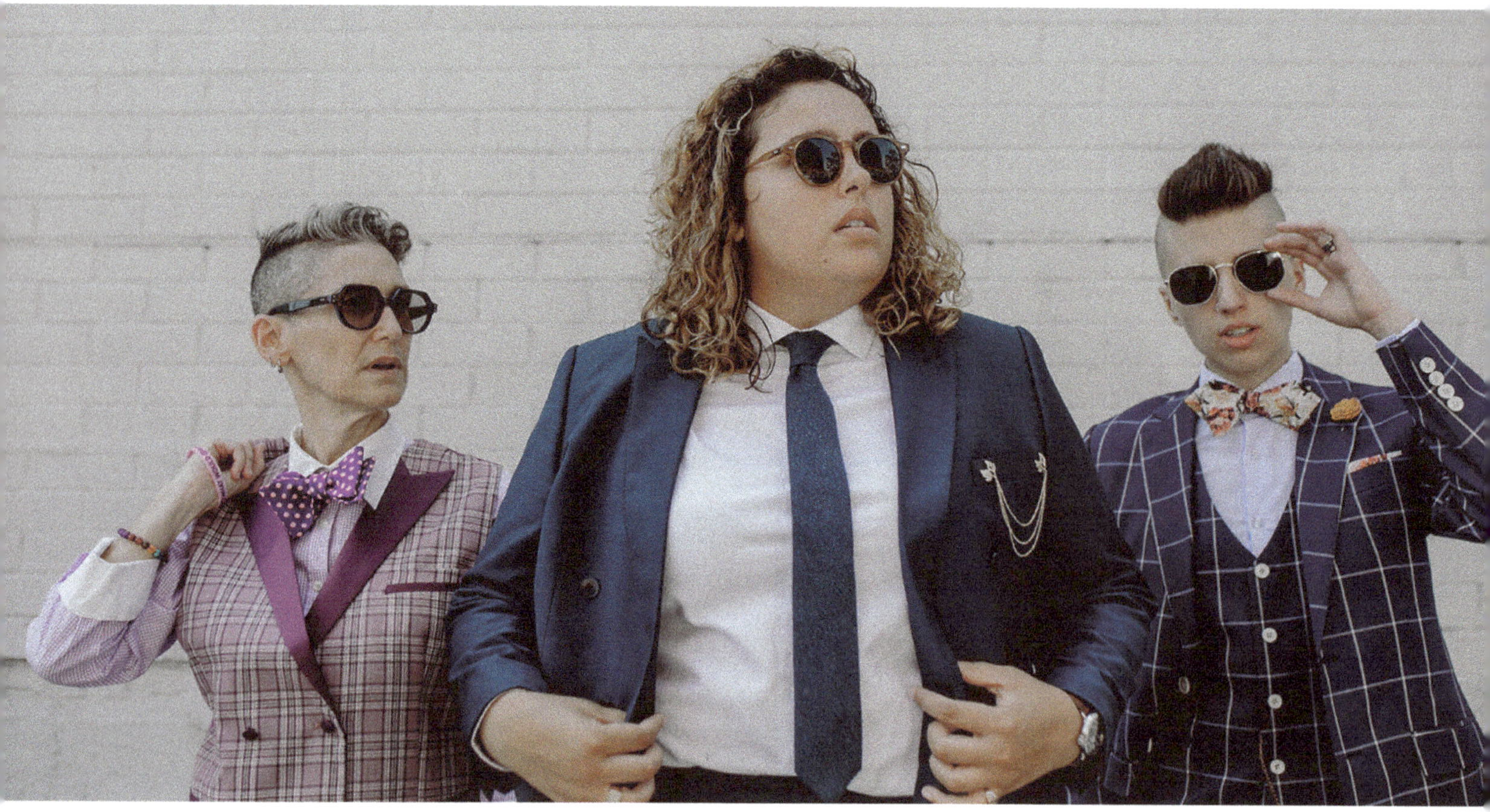

ShaneAve.
SYDNEY

LEADERS IN MADE TO MEASURE SUITS AND SHIRTS FOR EVERYBODY

FREEDOM OF EXPRESSION

www.shaneave.com   Instagram | @shane.ave   Facebook | @aveshane1

ALEX & DELANEY
Photography by Dewitt For Love, www.dewittforlove.com

The short and boring version is that they met at work. The longer, more interesting version involves a super sneaky three-month courting, a plethora of personal coffee and tea deliveries via skateboard, and some behind-the-scenes conversations with Delaney's best friend.

Before they could worry about what the world would think, they had to concern themselves with what their workplace would do if they found out about them because fraternization was not allowed in their employee conduct contract.

For three months, Alex arrived to work early enough to grab a good space in the parking garage and would skateboard downtown to the coffee shop, because who doesn't like a delish treat waiting on their desk when they arrive at work?

The first week she was a ball of anxiety trying to impress Delaney with different coffee blends, only to learn that she prefers tea. Majesty Mint tea is forever etched into Alex's brain now- oh joy.

Alex's efforts continuing throughout the second and third week made Delaney interested enough to agree to go to lunch together. Lunch each Friday then turned into lunch together almost every day, during the second month. Later, in that second month Alex had the most embarrassing dating moment when they showered Delaney in lemonade from laughing so hard at something she said. Her reaction (Delaney died, laughing of course) and coaching Alex through cleaning up enough to return to work, showed Alex they already had a positive connection.

Even with the gazillion hours a day they spent together, Alex still had to leave Delaney a letter asking to 'talk about us'. The plan was to ask her out nicely, but if you know Delaney, you know she has to address a potential issue IMMEDIATELY. So, on the spot, Alex expressed their interest more clearly and it turned out, the feeling was mutual.

In the third month, they transitioned into 'actual' dates and getting to know each other on a deeper level outside of jokes, hobbies, and commonalities. And. On December 28th, 2015, Alex asked Delaney to be their girlfriend and she FINALLY said yes.

A year ago now they married. It's gone a whole lot quicker than they imagined. And, creatively, they look at it like they've shared a year-long honeymoon thanks to arriving back from their actual honeymoon just before work from home orders were put in place and the pandemic really started to take hold.

For Alex and Delaney, it has been a year of learning about one another more every single day, a year of falling more and more in love, a year of creatively Covid-safe adventures with their soul mate.

Marriage is a long hallway full of framed iconic moments that they've shared together as a power couple and the challenges that they've overcome to become more united. They see communication ease, security, support, and unconditional love allowing their marriage to last the test of time. They want to be that annoying couple that finishes each other's sentences or communicates just with a look in a room full of people.

Creative. Heartfelt.
For the wildly in love.

www.daisyandpineweddings.com
@daisyandpinewedding

A TEN YEAR LOVE STORY
Photography by Mari Sabra Photography, www.marisabraphotography.com

I'm not sure how you collapse fourteen years into a story but here's the very, very short version..

Fourteen years ago on Halloween, Rachel and I met, through mutual friends, at the USF dorms in St. Pete. Well, 'met'- sort of. No one actually introduced us, but Rachel made a comment to me, I commented back, and then we went our separate ways. Afterward, a friend of mine immediately said, "You're going to date Rach!"

I thought in the back of my mind, "Date? .. I'm going to marry that girl."

We found each other on MySpace. Yes, MySpace. We realized that we were already friends on there. We exchanged numbers and after no rules, no holds, all cards on the table- about a week later we went on our first date. On November 8th we made it official. We were driving in the car listening to Otis Redding, and Rach looked at me and said, "So are we together or what?" .. An easy, "Yes" from me followed.

Rach proposed to me in New York City nine months later. Again an easy, "Yes" from me. When Rachel and I got engaged, LGBTQ+ marriage wasn't legal nationwide. We talked about flying to California to get married where it was legal [momentarily] and then that got overturned. So, we waited. Two years later my grandparents offered to host our wedding in Connecticut.

At the time, our marriage happened to be legal there. That's not why we ended up having the wedding there, but it was the perfect bonus.

We did all of the stuff we wouldn't have gotten to do in another state, which made it all the more special- we went to the courthouse and got a marriage license. We even saw a priest prior to the wedding- per my grandparent's request. He approved, and blessed our union. He actually married us, wearing a rainbow sash and all. He was so incredibly wonderful.

Our wedding was pure magic. Our photographer said at one point that she could feel the ground moving under her feet because every single person was on the dance floor. Every table was empty and although it wasn't planned, Pink's song 'Raise Your Glass' became the anthem of the night. It was an evening filled with so many feels- but mostly love, support and fun. We had the time of our lives.

We live in Florida, so when we returned home our marriage wasn't recognized. We actually tried to change our names when we returned home. Federally, it was recognized so our social security cards were changed. But then, we were denied by the DMV by a sincerely homophobic staff member. We fled to social media and our friends and family flooded the news stations with messages and phone calls. The story was initially covered by a local news station, but a few weeks later, the Tampa Bay Times published a story. The story is a testament to where things were- and that was just ten years ago. He untangled all of the realities surrounding LBGTQ+ couples who sought marriage. That was definitely a wake-up call, even to us- as youngsters: there was so much work to be done still.

When DoMA was overturned a few years later, we celebrated again (2013). And on that same date two years after that, marriage equality passed for the entire nation (2015). So, on June 26th, every year, we open a bottle of champagne.

It makes us smile that it all happened in the midst of Pride Month.

We have had quite the journey. We were 21 and 23 when we met. And, in 2021, we celebrate our ten year wedding anniversary. Our families celebrate holidays together. We help each other continue growing as humans. We have fur babies that fill our souls, and more love for one another than we could have imagined one life holding.

We are extremely blessed...lucky. Whatever you want to call it- we are just simply grateful beyond measure.

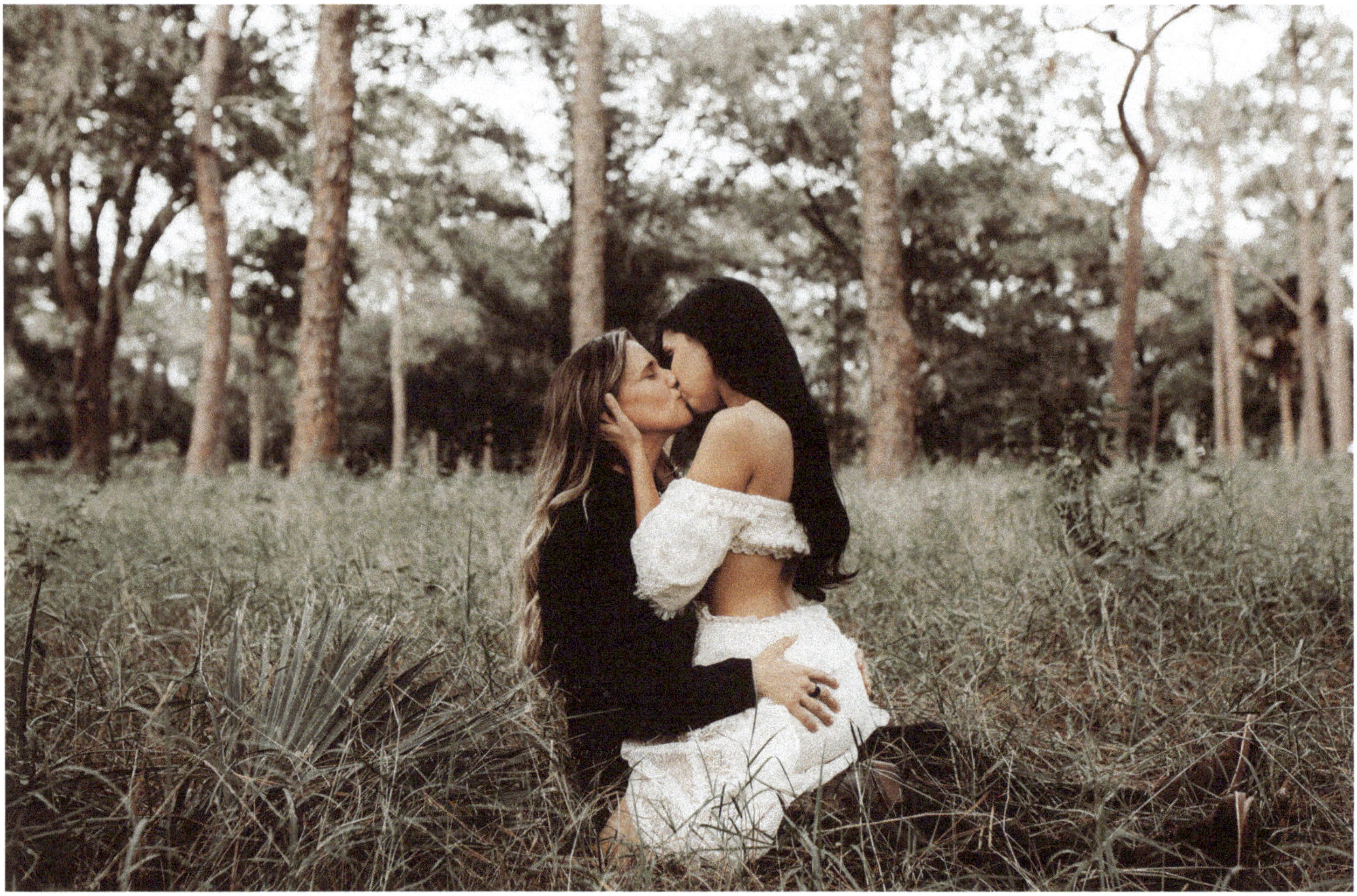

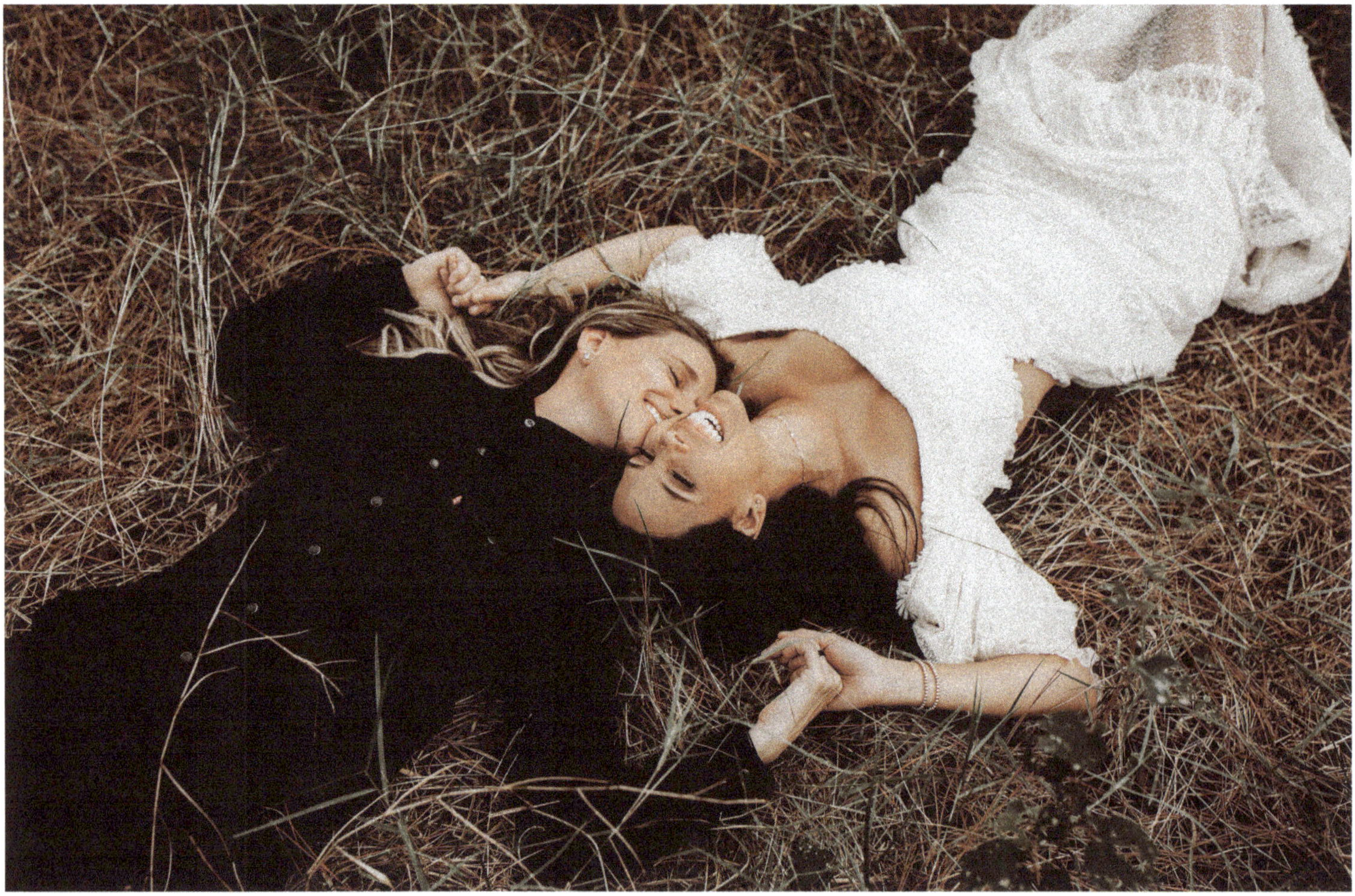

CLAIRE & KRIS - A CELESTIAL INSPIRED INTIMATE AFFAIR
Photography by Jennifer See Studios, www.jenniferseestudios.com

Even with a bunch of mutual friends, Claire and Kris' paths never really crossed. That was until one night, eighteen months after Claire had moved to Stratford, Ontario.

Claire was at a bar with friends; laughing and having fun, when she happened to look across the room and lock eyes with a certain human. Claire, who was blushing at this point, exclaimed to her friends, "Oh my gosh, I think that human over there is checking me out!" But, nothing really happened from there and they both went about their nights.

It turns out that so many missed opportunities to actually meet one another would follow.

Months later a mutual friend suggested that Claire host some drawing classes that Kris was bringing together. Eventually, the two would meet.

At first, it was professional. But as they kept meeting between the galleries and artist circles, collaborating and creating together. Eventually, Claire would become unsure of how to process the feelings she was having. Kris' energy, talent, and beauty was amazing. To her, it felt like she'd know them for a long time.

After a month of crossing paths more often, Claire took a friend to one of Kris's improv shows.

Kris got distracted watching Claire arrive late, they even took off their glasses as not to be distracted. They hung out after the show, continuing to set up their drawing class the next night. It got late, and as they were leaving they hugged goodnight.

There was a magnetic energy between them, and naturally flowed was a perfect first kiss.

Their relationship has inspired them both to understand true love. They didn't fall in love with each other based on a stereotype, expectation, or gender. They fell in love seamlessly and effortlessly.

They are creative business partners and life partners. Together Claire and Kris create arts media and events together which creates some incredible memories. And, while they are both happy leading busy lives, it's the downtime together that's really special. Some of their favorite moments together have been camping in the summer, without technology or work, just soaking in nature and on another.

For Claire, she is continually inspired and in awe of Kris's patience and kindness - with others and themself. And, for Kris, it's the way Claire unapologetically maneuvers through life with deserving confidence and respect for life at its essence- spiritually and ethically.

Moving forward, Claire and Kris continue to be inspired to create together, and are working towards some big projects together. Growing together, personally and professionally, always feels new and exciting.

Spring isn't the prettiest of seasons in Ontario, Canada, but that's exactly what inspired this styled intimate wedding.

The earthy, murky color palette that the creatives saw outside of their windows brought to life indoors.

Local flowers that were both attainable in terms of season and location, were brought together by The Little Flower Shed Co. A perfect blend of texture, drama and magic.

Small celestial nods created a 'larger than life' love story. The idea that the universe is on our sides as we connect with people who are meant to help us grow and evolve and love in ways we could never have imagined inspired the details. Stained glass moons for place settings, small gold star confetti scattered across the tables, moon necklaces, a vintage wooden moon tray for the ceremony lounge and moon and star headpieces are just a few of the elements that brought this aspect together.

Orbe lamps on the dining table added a romantic atmosphere - a unique style of lamp not often seen at weddings. The perfect accent to the candles that sprawled across the floors, tables, and window sills.

Smaller weddings don't always need to be just some chairs in a row or guests standing in a circle, and this is proof of that. A cozy lounge to relax in while you read your vows, make your promises, and seal your commitment can be just as intimate.

Catering The Ktchn | **Decorative Elements & Stationery** SB Creative Studio | **Dress Boutique** Fitzroy Rentals | **Florist** The Little Shed Flower Co | **H&MU** Jordan Ashley | **Photographer** Jennifer See Studios **Venue** Up Country Venues

ALICIA & PAVITHRA

PHOTOGRAPHY BY SARAH MCCLURE PHOTO
www.sarahmcclurephoto.com

SALT LAKE CITY, UNITED STATES OF AMERICA

It hasn't always been a smooth road for Alicia and Pavithra. Working through the trauma of being unaccepted in their relationship has been challenging. They each grew up in conservative communities - Alicia as a Mormon in Idaho, Pavithra as a Hindu in India. And, although many of the people in their lives have become more accepting in time, it's still an obstacle they face.

They also spent the first year of their relationship long-distance, which comes with its own heartache and challenges.

As they fell in love, Alicia was reminded of Pavithra's bravery. Knowing that she came out in India, where at the time even being queer was illegal made her heart full with pride. There aren't words for 'gay' or 'lesbian' in Pavithra's native language, yet this woman was so strong in her identity.

For Pavithra, it was Alicia's goofiness that really drew her in. Alicia has a way of lightening the mood and making Pavithra laugh, a shared humor that they both feel is the stronghold in their relationship.

They feel so lucky to have one another.

Eventually, Alicia would sell her home in Utah, pack up her car and drive across the country to be with Pavithra in Boston.

There were two proposals that would follow. Alicia knew that she wanted to incorporate their shared love for stars into a proposal somehow. She found a little observatory in Rhode Island and planned to keep it simple - head to a stargazing event and find a spot on the grounds to get down on one knee.

However, the day before the planned proposal, the observatory closed down indefinitely due to Covid. Not deterred, Alicia packed some binoculars, red lights and a star chart and drove out anyway. They had the entire grounds to themselves. As they lay on a blanket talking and stargazing the time felt right. She got up, got down on one knee and asked Pavithra to marry her.

Pavithra incorporated another shared love - food shows. She chose one of their favorite chefs and booked a date for dinner. She wrote Alicia a love letter and got dressed up for dinner. As they were getting ready for entree, Pavithra got down on one knee and proposed to her wife with the letter.

When it came to wedding planning they knew that they wanted to have an Indian-American fusion. Pavithra wanted to incorporate the Indian tradition of Saptapadi (seven promises) into the vows. Alicia also chose to surprise her bride by setting up thoranams (mango leaf arches) at the entrance - traditionally they're believed to keep negative energy away from the venue.

They both wanted to wear their white dresses for the ceremony to honor Alicia's traditions, then wear Indian lehengas for the reception. It meant for two particularly emotional first looks, both captured by Sarah McClure Photo.

It was a perfect day and they were surrounded by their closest family and friends. The six hours they spent celebrating felt as if it had flown by in mere minutes. During speeches those closest to the newlyweds shared sweet memories from the past and celebrations, food and sweets went well into the evening.

And, for a grand send-off, they had their guests form an arch with sparklers lit. A perfect end to start the next chapter of their lives together.

Cake THE CHOCOLATE, A Dessert Cafe | **Catering** Culinary Crafts | **Dress Boutique** Madeleine's Daughter Bridal | **Engagement & Wedding Rings** Sophie Hughes | **Florist** Urban Chateau Floral | **Furniture Hire** Alpine Rentals | **Hair** Madi Richmond | **Henna** Mountain Mehndi | **Lighting & Sound** Charisma Event Productions | **Makeup** Marisa Rose | **Photographer** Sarah McClure Photo | **Place Cards** Print-Mark | **Stylist** Canvas Wedding & Events | **Venue** Wadley Farms

Wedding Films and Love Stories Captured Forever

Tell us about your day
hello@nativeweddings.com.au
nativeweddings.com.au
+61 498 847 265

© Photo Credit www.nikiphoto.com.au

ANGIE & LAURA
PHOTOGRAPHY BY AMORVINCITOMNIA
www.ritafoldi.com

VENICE, ITALY

They met on a dating site and after a few days had passed, Angie asked Laura to meet with her only realizing as she saw the beautiful girl outside the cafe that she never had mentioned her name.

They walked along the perimeter of the castle of Castelfranco. Angie was rather annoying this particular afternoon, and after staying out far too late the night before- the date ended with her falling asleep. Not a fabulous start to a relationship. Angie often wonders what prompted Laura to call her back.

Some of their favorite memories are those that built the strong foundation of friendship. Exploring new cities together, sharing art and laughing.

Angie recalls one particular night during a walk in Bassano where Laura announced that she was sorry that there was nothing romantic building between them- everything initially was just a friendship. Angie gave her her jacket, and remembers how natural it felt.

It was in that moment, Angie realized that she didn't need any grand gestures to get Laura to see her in a romantic light, rather all she needed was to be herself. Eventually, Laura would fall in love and the friendship they'd built would just be the foundations of something spectacular.

Despite Angie dreaming of a classic Disney fairytale, movie-inspired, proposal, there wasn't really a marriage proposal. In fact, there wasn't even an engagement ring. Angie and Laura had been talking about weddings for a period of time and one evening at dinner while discussing their eventual marriage, Angie asked Laura why these plans couldn't be a reality. On the same wavelength, it was a mutual yes.

Venice was always a place that Angie wanted to elope. It's the place where she's spent some of her best years. Creatives at heart, the brides collaborated with Hecate Events to recreate a bucolic garden. An escape from reality, a world of their very own was created.

Of particular recognition, the florals by Frida's Venezia really brought to life the romantic feel that exudes from the intimate day.

The desserts were chosen for both taste and aesthetic, and stationery, by The Creative Design Lab, inspired by Fragonard's 1767 oil painting, 'The Lucky Chances of the Swing'. What became was something far more magical than either bride could have dreamt up.

Laura describes the day much like she describes her now-wife; full of love, bright and radiant.

They chose to read personal vows under a floral pavilion and exchanged rings as they made their promises.

Choosing to elope was an easy decision. It had been clear since the day they met that their connection was one that would be forever lasting.

Telling their friends and family was met with a resounding cheer. They each had the blessing of those dearest to them, Angie's grandmother cried with happiness. They each feel loved, and are forever grateful for that.

As they look into the future, they're doing so dubiously- the only thing certain is that they'll be standing together, side by side. They dream of owning a little house together that becomes their nest. Somewhere to furnish themselves and make feel like home.

One step at a time.

Desserts Pasticceria Alvaro Bido | **Florist** Frida's Venezia | **Gown Boutique** Ariel Spose | **Gown Designers** Made With Love Bridal, Emmy Mae Bridal **H&MU** Letizia Cordella | **Photographer** AmorVincitOmnia | **Planner** Hecate Events | **Stationery** The Creative Design Lab | **Venue** Ca' Nigra Lagoon Resort Venice | **Videographer** Your Creative Film | **Wedding Rings** L'unica Venezia

RUPERT

www.rupertonrupert.com.au
@rupertonrupert

UNPLUGGED WEDDINGS
and why you might just want to explore the option.

Having guests be present, and not distracted, is the main reason that you might go down the route of an unplugged wedding. That and the fact that you've hired a professional photographer to document the day - you really don't need Uncle Jim getting in their way.

So often we spend important moments actually behind the lens of a camera trying to capture the moment rather than encapsulating ourselves in the actual experience. Your wedding day doesn't have to be another one of missed moments.

An unplugged wedding is when you ask your guests to not take photos during your wedding. You might choose to include that rule across the entire wedding day, or just host an unplugged ceremony.

By asking your guests to keep their phones in their pockets, you're both guaranteed to have them present during the important moments, and not have them ruin the professional photographers shots. Let's be honest, you want to see their faces in your photos and not the backs of their phones!

And, communicating your desires for an unplugged wedding doesn't have to be daunting, we promise.

Tell them on the invite
Be upfront and set up your expectations from the very beginning - this might be on a paper invite, or on your wedding website.

Wedding Signage
Usually, a sign that's visible as guests walk into your ceremony location or venue works best.

Have your celebrant or officiant announce it
As the ceremony begins, they can let your guests know your wishes, and to keep their phones in their pockets.

There are lots of fun ways to tell your guests about it too- don't be shy to inject your personality into it. It certainly isn't an announcement that has to come across like you're laying down the law.

Phrases like these might work for you;

- We've hired an incredible photographer to capture every aspect of our day- please, keep your camera in your pocket.

- We ask that you are present with us as we make our commitment to one another. Please let our photographer take the only photos today.

- We want to see your beautiful faces in our photos when we look back at our wedding photos, without the distraction of your phone or cameras. Please put away your phone.

- We've chosen to have an unplugged wedding. Please keep our ceremony camera-free. We promise to share the photos once we've got them.

CAITLIN & FRANCES
PHOTOGRAPHY BY SHANE SHEPHERD
www.shaneshepherd.com

BRISBANE, AUSTRALIA

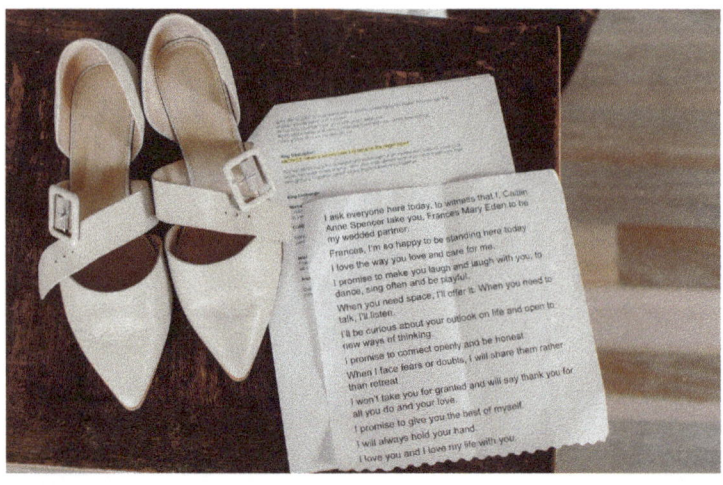

Why marry? We are asked, 'Why...why decide to get married after twenty years together?'

Seventeen years ago, three years into our relationship, we shopped in Sydney for commitment rings. We recall how uncomfortable we felt ringing the buzzer to enter the jewelry shops. We had to lay our relationship on the table. 'We're here to look at commitment rings, for each other.'

Back then, even in Sydney, it took the jeweler a minute or two to understand we were together, and work out how to approach us. We didn't fit into their standard business model. It wasn't the joyful experience we wanted. So, we waited another year until the energy was right and found lovely antique rings in Brisbane. Now that was beautiful: the rings had a story, a uniqueness: we could relate to that.

Forward to today, and we had a perfect wedding ring purchasing experience and have been able to formalize our relationship with a public marriage ritual that has offered such joy. We're proud that we have stepped out of our protected cocoon and declared our love. It is not just liberating, it's emotionally overwhelming.

That aside, a major reason to marry after twenty years is to celebrate the journey we have had so far.

As part of our wedding preparation, we sat with a bottle of wine and recalled our most important journey decisions so far; the decisions that tested and strengthened our bond.

The first big decision was made in the Brisbane Botanical Gardens in 2002. We had only just started going out. We had both been offered promotions in Sydney. Should we move to Sydney together and share a place? It was a big decision as we were very new. It was basically a decision to move in with a new partner after eight weeks together. We decided to be brave, trust each other, and take the leap of faith. This decision is why we are still together. We knew no one in Sydney and relied heavily on each other, so became a team.

We learnt to listen, to be honest and patient. There was nowhere to run to when things got tough; when our differences and individual needs started to show. The isolation of Sydney both forced and enabled us to get to know each other: this was both confronting yet fabulously decadent.

The second biggest decision was to return to Brisbane. After we worked our way 'out of our early relationship bubble, our values were clarified, and we knew we wanted to come home to support family; especially to be Aunties. We wouldn't be the fulfilled people who we are today if we were still spending our time trying new funky Sydney restaurants, drinking Bloody Mary's at Bondi and shopping on Oxford street.

The third biggest decision? To have a child. Being parents has both tested and strengthened our relationship. There's no doubt that it changed our dynamic; parenting takes whilst it gives, but it gives more. We've slowly, and purposefully, moved to a different version of 'us'; an us with Johnny, which we love.

It's been a journey, one that we've both had to change for, yet we've always carved out time to put our relationship first; to ensure we remain the 'Fraitlin' team. It takes work to stay connected and listen amongst the noise, but the fact that we're now married, so full of joy, proves it's worth it and we're excited to see what our future holds.

A large part of holding our wedding was to say thank you – to family and friends, for being there for us. You listened when we were confused. Shared stories when we craved connection. Entertained when we needed to laugh. Held us when we needed strength. And celebrated with us when life gave us joy.

Cake Secret Weapon Cakes | **Catering & Venue** Harvest Newrybar | **Celebrant** Michelle Shannon | **Dress Boutique** Babushka Ballerina | **Dress Designer** Wendy Makin Bridal | **Entertainment** Franky Smart | **Florist** Victoria Fitzgibbon | **H&MU** Jen Carlson | **Photographer** Shane Shepherd | **Signage & Stationery** The Paper Empire | **Wedding Rings** Canturi

JUSTINE & SARAH

PHOTOGRAPHY BY JACQIE Q PHOTOGRAPHY
www.jacqieq.com

COOPER'S ROCK STATE PARK, UNITED STATES OF AMERICA

After meeting in the emergency department while working, Justine and Sarah dated for a little over a year before Justine asked Sarah to be her wife.

While backpacking in the Linville Gorge Wilderness they'd just finished setting up camp for the night when Justine mentioned that she had a surprise. Expecting dessert or a cold beer, Sarah unzipped the tent door to see Justine down on one knee on the edge of the gorge.

It was an easy 'yes'.

They spent the next eight months engaged.

Wedding planning wasn't exactly what they'd dreamt of. Covid impacted the planning and foregoing a large wedding celebration, the couple decided to have only their parents present at their wedding ceremony and let go of plans to have a reception.

Being active outdoors; hiking, biking, camping, cross-country skiing, and kayaking, is important to the couple. And, these hobbies influenced their decision to lust for an outdoor ceremony at sunrise. They went with a casual, laid-back vibe. Coopers Rock State Forest is a special place to Justine and Sarah, they spend a lot of time there and feel like it's a beautiful representation of their state, West Virginia. It was the perfect spot to become married.

With Mother Nature, in all their incredible beauty, responsible for all the decor, Justine and Sarah simply packed a brunch picnic to celebrate in a nearby pavilion after their ceremony.

The first thing of the day was revealing to each other their BHLDN gowns for the very first time. An emotional moment for both brides. A moment that they both would look back on as their favorite moment from the day.

They had traveled to Pittsburgh, Pennsylvania together with Justine's sister to try on dresses at BHLDN. Justine had found her dress that day, and Sarah ended up ordering hers online a few weeks later. Their dresses were both sleek and fitted, completely complimentary.

At sunrise, as the fog was rolling through the valley each of their parents walked them down a rock path aisle, 'Here Comes the Sun' by The Beatles playing in the background. Justine and Sarah exchanged conversational vows that they wrote together overlooking the picturesque valleys of Coopers Rock State Forest. And, while their parents were the only people present physically, there was a live stream on Facebook so that all of their family and friends could watch from home.

Then, they went to that pavilion. Cut quiche in lieu of cake and ate cinnamon rolls. They danced, had a fire, and enjoyed both the simplicity of their day and the commitment that they'd just promised to one another.

Looking back there is nothing that they'd change, aside from having their siblings there in person if they could. In saying that, the newlyweds are both incredibly grateful to have had the opportunity to have their family and friends there, albeit virtually.

For Justine and Sarah marriage is always being on the same team and supporting each other. It's finding comfort in each other's presence and living life with your best friend.

Cake Casselman Cafe | **Catering** Terra Cafe | **Ceremony Venue** Cooper's Rock State Park | **Cinematographer** Lady Mountain Films | **Dress Boutique** BHLDN | **Engagement Rings** Jacqueline's Fine Jewelry | **Florist** Rooted By Design | **Photography** Jacqie Q Photography

JENNIFER MOHER

...documenting the essence of the human soul and the beautiful connections that exist between us

WWW.JENNIFERMOHER.COM

@JENNIFERMOHER

MAR & XIOMARA
Photography by Lorena León, www.lorenaleon.com
Officiant María Lorian, www.marialorian.com

Just a year after their love story began, Madrid witnessed the love Mar and Xiomara have for each other. They started by saying 'I do' to each other in Madrid's Chueca station and continued until sunset in another corner of Madrid.

Of course, there was a proposal before any of this came to life.

Leading up to the moment of the proposal, Mar started to tremble and seemingly couldn't find words. She just looked at the human she'd fallen in love with, at the very same table where they had shared their first dinner date together, chest exploding with love.

It's hard to recall the moment. Xiomara had no idea what was going on, but as she started putting things together it felt like she was a part of the best romance film made. With their closest friends and family watching on a video call, she said 'yes' to Mar.

They had every reason to elope. Marriage was important to fulfill before they moved forward with plans to start a family and the pandemic meant that they wouldn't be able to have a 'traditional' wedding anyway.

A simple, but meaningful union on the streets of Madrid was a perfect fit for Mar and Xiomara.

In complementing taupe suits and no other styling, Mar and Xiomara wed. Focusing wholly on their love and their vows to each other for a healthy and loving future.

To the newlyweds, marriage is saying good morning to one another for every sunrise that they have left to live. They make one another better people by enhancing their best qualities and virtues.

The world stands still when Mar and Xiomara look into the eyes of each other. Vanishing are thoughts of insecurities - their relationship has no space for them.

Eventually, when the world calms down they dream of having a bigger wedding. They have incredible support from their families and they can't wait to be able to celebrate their love and commitment with them. Until then, they dream of a future together that's filled with respect, love, empathy, support, stability, and happiness. A future where, despite life's ups and downs, together they are able to guide and support each other.

HOW TO CHOOSE YOUR WEDDING VENDORS
the VIP's that bring your wedding day to life

You're engaged! Congratulations!

Now, it's time to head down the rabbit hole of finding the perfect wedding suppliers to help bring to life what you envision your wedding day will be.

Which sounds fun, right? Until you realize that there are literally thousands of wedding pros out there to choose from - and it can get confusing.

From photographers to florists, event planners to the stationery designers, it can get overwhelming quickly - so, here's a little step by step guide to ease your way through the process.

1. Take your time
You're engaged, enjoy that bubble of excitement! There's no reason to jump onto locking in your vendors before you have done your homework. Celebrate being newly engaged with your lover - you deserve that. Go on dates, throw that engagement party and know that wedding planning will come in time.

2. Do your research
First things first, think about where you want to get married, the style and vibe you want the day to have and map out your budget.

The best way to go about this is to each sit-down and think about the three things you want to prioritize for your day - it might be photography, your wedding outfits, and your venue. Keep these at the top of your mind when you are looking for vendors.

Find vendors through magazines, blogs, social media or word of mouth. Head to expos, if that is your scene.

3. Send you inquiries
Get your information ready and reach out to the wedding vendors who have made your 'we need to know more' list. You'll need; your names, contact details, wedding date, wedding location, and any questions that you want to ask.

Your initial inquiry is a good opportunity to see if you vibe with the wedding pro, make sure that they work within your budget, and that they are available on the date you're hoping to marry.

4. Shortlist your vendors
If you've reached out to three different florists, it's now time to cull that list down to two (or one, if you can!).

If you have only reached out to one stylist who you're head over heels in love with, and you don't want to consider anyone else, it's totally okay to skip ahead and make a decision. Don't feel like you need to complicate things.

5. Arrange consultations
If you are having trouble really narrowing down your list, it might be time to book in for a face-to-face (or online/phone) consultations.

While it might not be necessary to arrange a consultation with all of your wedding vendors, we would recommend really catching up with your photographer and officiant at the very minimum. These are two wedding vendors that are going to play one of the most significant roles on your wedding day. You want these people to really understand your love story, and champion it.

6. Make your decisions
The most exciting part - it's time to lock in your chosen wedding vendors. Make sure you get in touch as soon as you've made a decision so that your wedding date is still available. It is commonplace that you'll need to pay a deposit before you can confirm your booking.

Before you do pay that deposit, it's your last chance to read over contracts and ask any questions.

You don't want to go into anything without knowing exactly where you stand.

And, it should go without saying, reach out to the wedding vendors who you have decided, for whatever reason, just aren't right for you. It's common courtesy. Don't stress about the wedding vendors taking offense; they will appreciate the honesty, we promise.

FRANCES & JESSIE

PHOTOGRAPHY BY FOX AND TWIG
www.foxandtwig.com

DELAWARE, AUSTRALIA

There are still two wedding dresses hanging in the rosewater room here at the farmhouse. The beautiful pink room that we painted together. This is where the dresses still hang. Neither of us ready yet to put them away.

Most of the wedding planning seemed to just happen. I do not specifically remember talking about many decisions, it was as if we both had the very same vision in our minds of what our day might be.

When we met, I lived on three acres in the country, an old farmhouse, and a huge barn. She lived in a flat in the city, an old brick building with a terrific front porch. That porch is where we fell in love.

Plans were intentional. We created little nodes, living rooms, spaces for gathering for all of our friends and family. We cleaned out the old barn and rid it of all kinds of varmints. We weeded garden beds. We hung lights high in the trees, we grew flowers, and had our friends doing the same. We borrowed enough kitchen chairs for everyone to have a seat in the barn for the ceremony.

We spent two years checking things off of our wedding plan. We worked on the weekends but set a time to stop work and enjoy what we had accomplished, to enjoy each other.

A fall wedding date was set when the sun would be shining and the temperature mild enough to not be cold in a sleeveless wedding dress, but cool enough to adorn some flannel shirts later in the evening. The corn across the street still stood tall. In a whirlwind event like a wedding, I think the little moments that speak to you are in the snippets of memory.

Seeing her in that beautiful dress for the first time, she said to me that she had to stop herself from running down the path to greet me. I love that. Her lipstick and the deep v-neck dress, my heart raced. We grabbed each other and then both stood back to take a better look.

Waiting for the ceremony to begin; deciding that it might be best to share a nip of bourbon together before we walk to the barn, we sat in the living room. We draped together as she continued to calm me. Then, it was time to put on our wedding boots and walk. When we practiced this, alone together, in our work clothes and gardening gloves, to our song, I cried even then. Through every moment, I am in awe that I get to marry her. In constant gratitude.

I remind myself that though she is mine and I am hers, we are both just borrowed, in a place where nothing should be assumed or taken for granted. We deserve each other because we earn each other over and over again.

The walk to the barn seems long now that I think back on it. She makes me pause midway between the house and the barn, look at her, take a breath. 'It is just me and you.' We breach the door of the barn. All of our friends are there. I grab her arm and remind her to stop at the door for a moment. We do. We kiss. Then, we walk. Approaching our parents, we hug them, they squeeze us. We stand on a Southwest-style rug that we bought specially for this day.

The ceremony is made up of everyone important in our lives each contributing something to us, writings, notes, poetry, stories, they all step up to read to us. Then, we turn and read to each other. Before we do, she turns around, looking slowly at everyone in attendance; her intentional way of pausing to be sure to remember this very moment. She reads first. She looks up and into my eyes. Then she slips that ring onto my finger. As she is reading, I am grinning, big. Grinning because there are so many things that she says to me, that I have also planned to say to her.

I read to her. I put her ring on her finger, as I did the day she said yes to me. In my mind, there is a valley-wide moment between the kiss and us walking out together as wives.

COVID
HOTEL

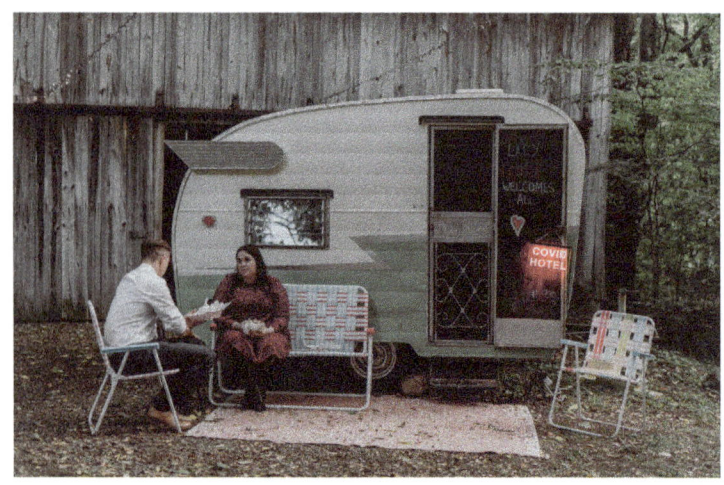

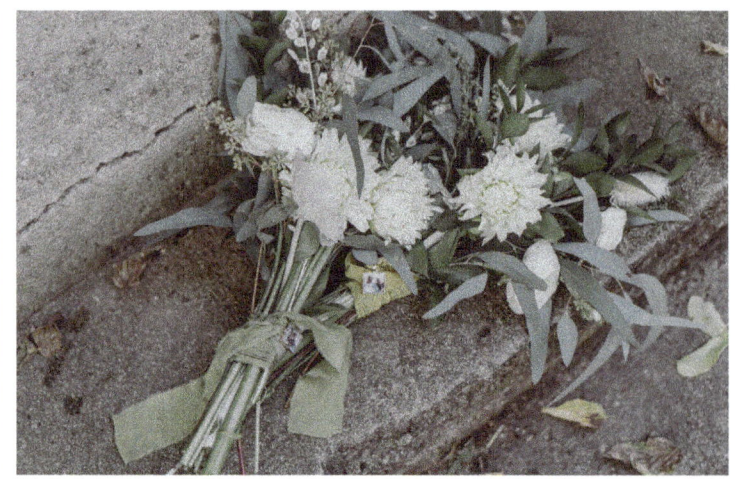

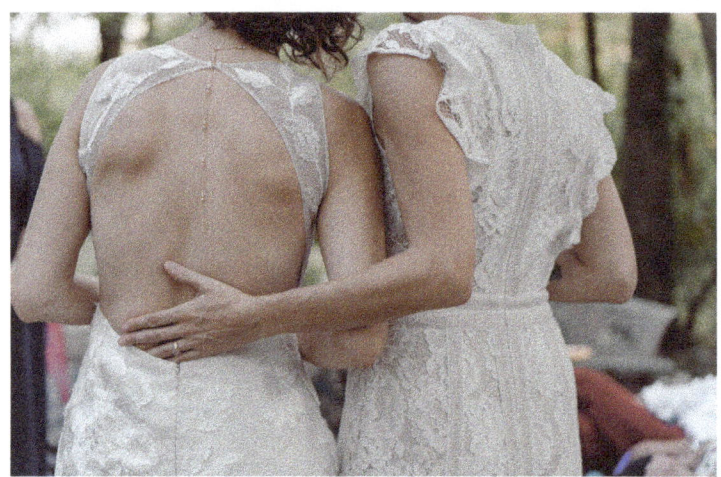

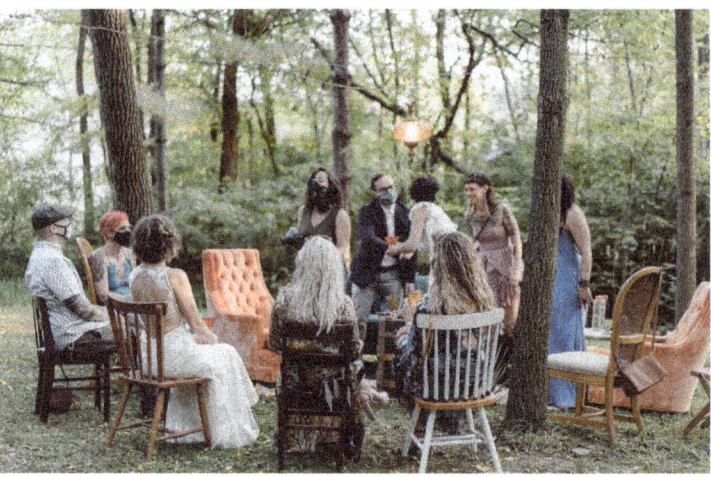

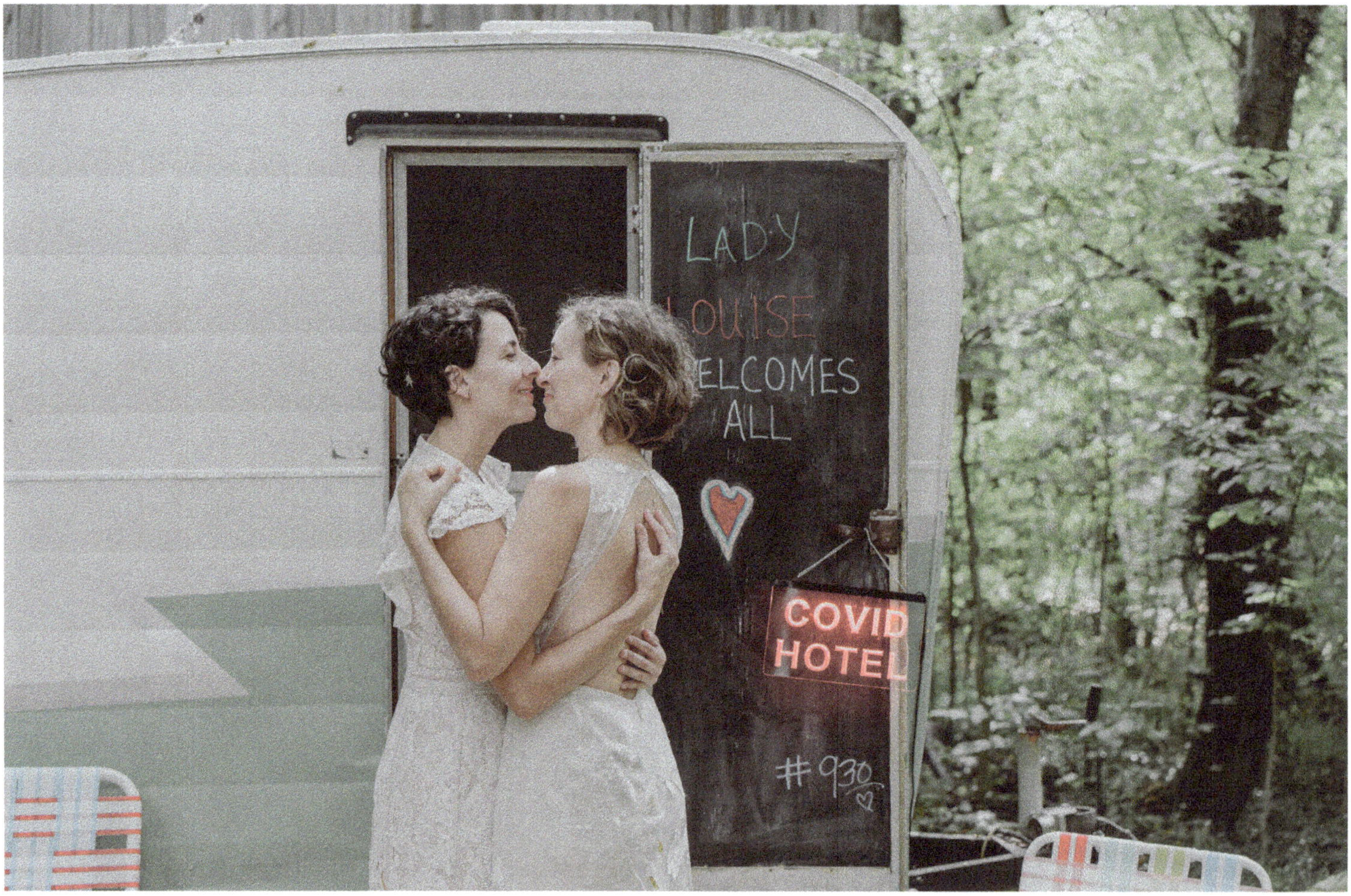
LADY
ALL
COVID
HOTEL
#930

Celebrants Lisa Ho, Jeremy Kerr | **Cinematographer** Adam Stiffler | **Engagement & Wedding Rings** Worthington Jewelers, Jared | **Entertainment** Mary Elaine | **Florist** Marti Babcock, Jay Waldron | **Food Trucks** Little Ladies Soft Serve, En Place | **Gown Boutique** BHLDN | **H&MU** Paul David Endicott | **Photographer** Fox and Twig | **Stationery** Whitespace | **Transport** River's Edge Native Trees and Nursery

A GUIDE TO WEDDING WEBSITES
for digital wedding invitations and organization

It's not uncommon to skip over traditional wedding invitations that get sent in the mail and opt into a wedding website instead. A digital invitation of sorts that has the ability to convey all of your wedding information, and then some, packaged neatly inside your own little space on the internet.

They're not for everyone, but they might be the solution you've been looking for.

PROS OF HAVING A WEDDING WEBSITE

- Environmentally friendly- there's no waste
- You'll save money- no postage budget needed
- You don't have to worry about things being lost in the post
- It can be really easy to DIY
- Information can be updated easily
- It's easy for your guests to RSVP
- Your wedding information is always accessible
- You can include more information than you would on a traditional invite
- It's easy to convey all of the information in one spot- multiple emails and phone calls aren't necessary

CONS OF HAVING A WEDDING WEBSITE

- It can be hard to access for guests who don't use the internet
- It can feel less personal, and less formal
- You'll need to be tech-savvy for personalization outside of the capabilities of the wedding website service
- You'll need your guests email addresses

HOW TO CREATE A WEDDING WEBSITE

A quick Google will bring up plenty of results- and there really isn't a 'one size fits all' option. These options all vary in price, and functionality. Shop around to find something that fits your budget, but also your skill level when it comes to building a website.

- Square-space
- Wix
- Say I Do
- Wed-sites
- Minted
- Joy
- Zola
- Appy Couple
- The Knot
- Riley and Grey

Photography by Conie Suarez Braro

WHAT TO INCLUDE ON YOUR WEDDING WEBSITE

If you've decided that creating a wedding website is for you, you'll want to keep a few things in mind when you're creating it. While this list of things to include might seem daunting, don't stress. Include only what's relevant to you. And, keep in mind that your guests will probably head to your website to RSVP, and then to find out the time and location details closer to the wedding date.

While writing an epic tale of all the details of your relationship so far might be really fun, focus on things that will be helpful to your guests first and foremost.

- Share a little about your story- it's a personal touch
- Where and when the wedding will take place- include the start time and location of both the ceremony and reception if they don't follow one another
- Contact information, just in case
- A way that your guests can RSVP and a date that it needs to be done by
- Space for guests to include dietary requirements or ask questions
- Information about wedding gifts- a link to your registry or a note saying that having them in attendance is the only gift you need
- Information about hotels in the area
- Directions to the venue and transport options
- If you've got a dress code, include that
- COVID-19 safe plan if your wedding is impacted by the pandemic
- If you're planning to live stream your wedding, include the information
- Any additional information that is specific to your event- let people know you are having a cash bar, or a kids-free event, or that you're having an unplugged ceremony, or details of a morning-after brunch if you've got something planned.

And, once all the important stuff is out of the way, a few optional extras might include:

- A space to make song requests
- An introduction to your wedding party
- Wedding day timeline
- A song playing in the background that is meaningful to your relationship
- Your wedding hashtag if you've got something you'd like to use

Photographer
Silk & Thorn
www.silkandthorn.com

Accessories Ash&Cort, Movado | **Bridesmen Outfits** Perfect Tux | **Cake** Cake Creations | **Catering** Abraham Catering | **Celebrant** Dominique Morgan | **Engagement & Wedding Rings** Greensberg Jewelers | **Entertainment** DJ Next One | **Florist** Loess Hills Floral | **Gown Boutique** Rhylan Lang Bridal | **Gown Designer** Made With Love Bridal | **H&MU** Sierra Parks, Rosha Taylor, Hair by Jasmine Brown | **Page Boy Outfits** H&M | **Photo Booth** Premier Party | **Planner & Stylist** 402Events | **Printer** Dana Osborne | **Shirt** ASOS | **Shoes** Nike | **Socks** Ralph Lauren | **Stationery** Sincerelybynicole | **Suit Designer** Afielda | **Transport** VIP Limousine | **Veil** Sara Gabriel | **Venue** The Aspen Room

CHARLENE & MARKIA
Photography by Silk & Thorn, www.silkandthorn.com

Five years ago, Charlene and Markia married in an intimate courthouse affair to save money while they were trying to conceive. By law, same-sex couples must be married to both be listed as parents on a birth certificate. They didn't even tell people that they were going down the marriage route.

Markia had proposed. She had planned a surprise party for Charlene's birthday and asked all of their friends and family to send across a video of why they love Charlene. Markia put those videos together and added an extra special one from herself to the very end.

As Markia's came on, Charlene began to cry and as it ended, she felt a tap on her should. Charlene turned around to see Markia on one knee asking her to marry her.

They'd picked the rings together, and talked about marriage, but it still came as a happy surprise.

A month after their courthouse wedding, Charlene fell pregnant. Although planned, it came unexpectedly. The doctor had suggested that they try before they were actually ready because the likelihood of everything going to plan the first time around was small.

Having a baby at the beginning of their marriage put a lot of strain on the couple. It didn't give them both the time to really enjoy the newlywed bubble and they soon separated. And, while they both spent that eight months apart knowing that they wanted to be with one another, coming back together was one of the hardest things that Charlene and Markia have had to do. They've both worked to make their relationship work.

Once they found themselves back together, they knew it was time to plan the big wedding that they had always dreamt of- mostly to celebrate with their friends and family. Their five-year anniversary was the perfect time to make that happen.

The day started off perfect, and then it began to rain. Some might say that's good luck, but Charlene and Markia weren't all that thrilled. Charlene's hair appointment also ran late, meaning the entire schedule of the day started on the back foot. Anxiety begun to creep in.

However, once they had their first look, everything came into place and the rest of the day flowed perfectly. Their wedding ended up being everything that the couple had dreamt it would be- and then a little more. From the decor, to the food. To their outfits and their guests. Everything was perfect.

Their guests agree, there's only one word to describe the day- unforgettable.

HOW TO HIRE ELOPEMENT WEDDING VENDORS

While it's not necessary to hire elopement-specific wedding vendors, it is something that you might want to consider- especially if you are planning to hike up a mountain and soak in incredible views while you say your vows.

Now, is this advice set in stone? No, you can absolutely hire any wedding professional to do any job for you. But, there are a few perks when it comes to hiring elopement-specific wedding vendors that you might not have thought over. Let's break it down and talk about the key wedding vendors that you'll be hiring to bring your elopement to life- and why you might want to consider those who specialize in elopements.

Photography by James White Photography

PHOTOGRAPHER

Usually, your photographer will be one of the first wedding professionals you hire- especially if you're eloping in nature. Hiring an elopement photographer, someone who has experience in the outdoors and someone who is great with adjusting to whatever weather presents on the day is going to be worth it.

An experienced elopement photographer will be knowledgeable about the locations that you might be looking at - they might even point you in the direction of some incredible spaces in nature that aren't often seen elsewhere. The kind of places that you wouldn't know about unless someone in the know lets you in on the secret. They'll also be mindful of the environment and the impact that your elopement will have on it.

Elopement photographers will usually be aware of local laws, particularly if you are planning to have a legal ceremony on the elopement day. Sometimes your photographer is the only person aside from the officiant to be present on the day and so you'll also be asking them to be a legal witness. Some photographers are even ordained, so they can perform the legal parts of the ceremony.

And, if you're not having an officiant present they will have experience in guiding an intimate elopement day, just the two of you.

OFFICIANT OR CELEBRANT

It's true that there are some places around the world where you do not need an officiant present to make your ceremony legal. However, these places are few and far between. If you plan to legally wed on your elopement day, you will need to plan to bring along an officiant or celebrant.

When it comes to your elopement officiant, you're going to want to find someone who you can connect with. An officiant who really spends the time getting to know you, your relationship, and is invested in supporting your decision to marry.

While you might be pressed to find an officiant who solely focuses on elopements, it might be handy to think about some questions to ask your officiant to get a feel about whether they're a good fit for your elopement. It would also be a good idea to ask the officiant if they are comfortable hiking and being outdoors, if you're planning an adventure elopement.

FLORIST

Whether you're planning to have a floral arch aside a clifftop, or you're looking for a simple bouquet that you're able to carry with you through a forest, finding a florist who can meet your needs is going to be really important.

Florals, as beautiful as they are, can be heavy and hard to transport and so, finding a florist who understands that you need something that will be easy to carry, if your hiking you'll need something that can be durable enough to last the hike and a florist who doesn't over promise because they don't quite understand how hard it really is to build an incredible arbor on the side of a mountain.

HAIR & MAKEUP

If this is a priority for you, it might be challenging to find an elopement-specific vendor for hair and makeup. However, there are plenty out there who will be up for the role. If you are planning something at sunrise, remember that hair and makeup will likely start well before the event- sometimes in the middle of the night. You'll want to connect with potential vendors and ask questions around their feelings about this. While they might be accustomed to early starts, something at 2 am might be a touch early!

PLANNER

For some, an elopement planner won't be necessary, however for others it will take a load off the stress of planning.

Usually if you've hired an elopement-specific photographer you'll find that they are able to take the reins when it comes to planning. Things like location, timeline and other wedding vendor recommendations are something they will likely handle as part of their services. It's always best to clarify with them if they're able to take on the extra responsibilities.

If you are having a small number of guests, or you just really like the idea of having an elopement planner some of the things that they might cover include: organizing your accommodations, transport, styling and setup on the day and coordinating details.

CALDER PHOTO

ELOPEMENTS + WEDDINGS

SMALL MOMENTS THAT CREATE THE BIG FEELINGS

WWW.CALDERPHOTO.COM   @CALDERPHOTOG

BOHO GLAM

Inspired to bring bohemian laid-back vibes together with a glimmer, or shimmer, of glam, this creative team brought to life natural earthy tones like terra cotta, tan, green and burgundy across this entire inspired wedding.

Couple, Candace and Delanie, stood in as models effortlessly in an incredible sequin jumpsuit and nude satin dress. Neither wore a veil, instead opting for a fedora with a Jardin Den Eden floral arrangement for one bride, a floral brooch for the other.

Both dry and fresh-cut florals were blended together perfectly across the ceremony scene and table scape. Knowing that a lot of couples don't have endless budgets for florals, Jardin Del Eden created an arrangement that was multi-use; used across the arbor during the ceremony and then transformed into a hanging installation for the reception.

Silk napkins, speckled plates, gold flatware and goblets from 3 Little Birds Event Planning dressed the table. The centerpieces were kept minimal, with candles and low vase flowers places across a macrame runner - proving that you don't always need more to create impact.

Photographer
Kristyn Taulane Photography
www.kristyntaulane.com

Cocktails Mixing in Action | **Cookies** Rachel Ansi | **Design** SBSN
Floral Jardine Del Eden | **Hair** Makeup by Sarah Kathleen | **Makeup** Kayla Arielle Artistry | **Planning** Kiss and Say I Do, SBSN | **Rentals** 3 Little Birds Event Planning | **Rings** Balacia | **Shoes** Bella Belle Shoes
Stationery Nicolette Martin Art | **Venue** La Canada Thursday Club
Videographer White Sparrow Weddings

LAUREN & TEEGAN

PHOTOGRAPHY BY DANI KNIGHT & CO
www.dkandcophotography.com

GOLD COAST, AUSTRALIA

Eight years ago Lauren and Teegan met through a mutual friend. While their mutual friend had thought they'd make excellent friends, they skipped over that part and started hanging out all the time.

They've built some incredible memories together, especially travelling. In 2019 they embarked on a six-month trip starting in Vancouver, Canada and ending in Chile, South America. There were ten countries along the way but their most memorable moment was the part when Lauren proposed at Machu Picchu.

Lauren had planned the proposal months before the big trip. They'd originally planned to propose within the first two weeks at Lake Loise, but it didn't work out as they both ended up with the flu and were too sick to make it happen. Instead, Lauren carried the ring with her around Central and most of South America waiting for the perfect moment to arise.

When Lauren and Teegan arrived at Cusco, in Peru, they organized to head up to Machu Picchu - Lauren had a feeling that it might be during this adventure that the time would feel right. So, they prepared themselves. The ring was hidden in the top of their jacket pocket, everything she was going to say saved into her phone.

It wasn't looking hopeful, it was a rather gloomy afternoon. So many clouds you could hardly see the ruins. After the tour everyone went their separate ways and Lauren and Teegan arrived at the viewing platform where hardly anyone was around. The clouds parted and they could suddenly see the ruins perfectly- 'this is it', thought Lauren.

They stood behind Teegan, and as they turned around, Lauren was there with a box to give her. None of the words Lauren had planned to say came out. It was hardly romantic but it was true to them. Teegan said 'yes!' And they were over the moon.

After their third wedding cancellation due to rolling lock downs, only a week out of their wedding day, their celebrant, Michelle from The Wild Hitcher, offered Lauren and Teegan the opportunity to elope instead. Teegan had always wanted to elope and so they decided they couldn't pass up the opportunity - especially with such uncertainty about going ahead with a fourth wedding date change.

It turned out that eloping was the best decision for them. They were able to have an intimate ceremony amongst nature - just the couple and their dog, Blue.

The morning of the elopement, Lauren and Teegan enjoyed a breakfast together. It was important to them to have that time to calm their nerves before the day ahead. The elopement day was perfect, sun shining.

Lauren and Blue arrived to the location before Teegan, they'd always wanted to do a first look and they're so grateful that they were able to make this a reality. It was the first moment they were able to see each other in their outfits. The ceremony was intimate and emotional- plenty of tears, laughter and happy dancing.

Family and friends understood the decision to elope, especially after everything that they'd gone through. They told their immediate family the day before the elopement who were happy for them, but also excited to really celebrate at the planned wedding party that they'd put together for later in the week. When it came to original guests and extended family and friends, Lauren and Teegan chose to let them know about their elopement the night after their ceremony.

Life ahead for Lauren and Teegan is something that's unknown, but they're both open to new ideas and adventures. They've just brought a home together and are spending plenty of time renovating that.

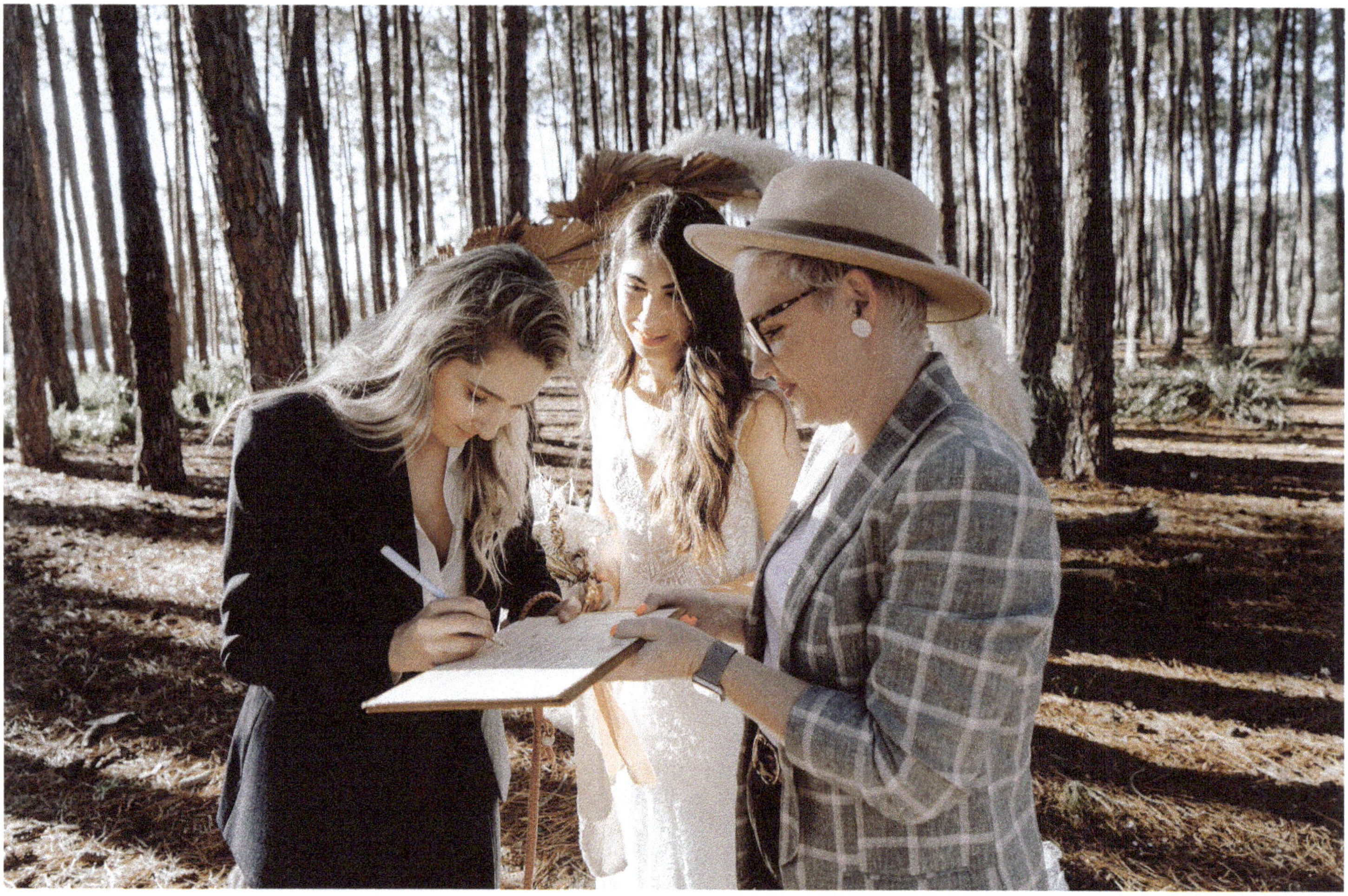

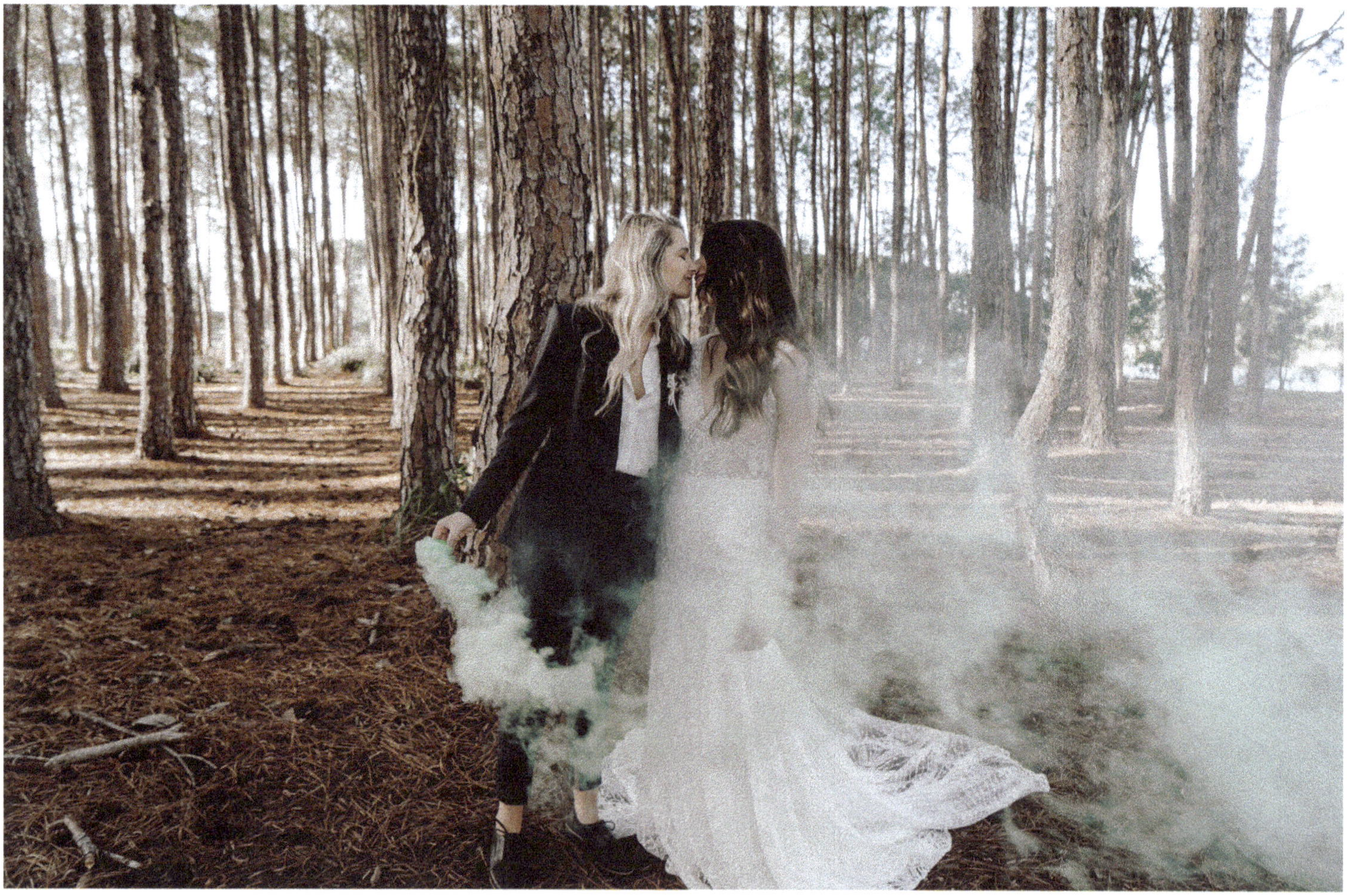

Celebrant & Planner The Wild Hitcher | **Ceremony Venue** Pizzey Park, Gold Coast | **Decorative Elements** Eco Confetti | **Dress Designer** GC Bridal Lounge | **Florist** Forever Us Events and Flowers | **H&MU** Georgia McAliece Hair | **Pet Accessories** Willows Way | **Photographer** Dani Knight & Co **Suit Designer** Effie Kats

Photography by Jonathan Borba

WHY YOU SHOULDN'T NEGOTIATE WITH YOUR WEDDING VENDORS

We get it, wedding budgets are often tight and often times we want just a little more bang for our buck, so to speak. And, wedding etiquette can be confusing to navigate. However, when it comes to negotiating prices with your wedding vendors- don't do it.

Now, we certainly don't mean that you shouldn't discuss your budget with your wedding vendors- you most definitely should. Sometimes those vendors will be able to work out a way that you're able to still work with them, often in a capacity less than what you might have had in mind originally. And, whether you're working with a planner or you've got yourself a trusty spreadsheet, there should always be an open discussion around adjusting your budget, especially if you have a particular vendor in mind that you really want to work with.

However, negotiating with wedding vendors is never recommended- they've set their prices, and asking them to change those devalue the cost of their services. Plus, it's not a nice way to start your client-vendor relationship. Even if you don't mean anything harsh when you do ask for a discount, it kind of comes across as, "the work you do, and your experience, is worth less than what you think it is," and that's not a nice pill to swallow.

Imagine asking your local restaurant for a discount when you receive the bill because you can't afford their prices- you just wouldn't!

Now, if you adore a particular wedding vendors work, but you're not sure if they'll be within your budget, it's easy to reach out and let them know upfront about your own budget. Let them know that you admire their work, and if they aren't able to meet your budget they might just be able to recommend another vendor that might.

Something to always keep in mind is this: most wedding vendors are small business owners. When you pay your invoices on time it helps keep all the cogs in their business and home lives moving forward- your payment helps that vendor put food on the table for the family and pay for their home, that, and all their business expenses.

And, with experience often comes a higher price point. For example, photographing a wedding is far different from just taking a few photos at a backyard birthday party. There are wedding day timelines, family dynamics to navigate, a list of images that the couple have requested to check off and often challenging lighting to work with. Knowing how to navigate all of this while being on your feet for 8+ hours, often without breaks comes with experience - and we've not even started to mention the hours they'll sit in front of a computer going through the thousands of photos to find the best ones to edit and present to you.

Expect to pay for the expertise and value that these wedding professionals will inevitably bring to your wedding experience.

So, how do you prepare to meet with vendors, knowing you won't negotiate prices?

Easy! First, research the market. Know roughly what a service might cost in the area you're searching. Having that expectation will help you plan a budget before you've reached out to anyone.

Also, have your wedding priorities handy. If, for example, having a videographer is important to you and wedding florals aren't, once you have got back some quotes you'll know where you can rearrange your budget. Maybe paying that little bit more for the videographer you really want, and cutting back to a basic wedding floral installation works for you.

And lastly, keep a budget! Don't forget to loop back to it at every point along the way. Keep conversations open, talk openly about your budget and plan your dream wedding - whatever it might look like for you!

A LUXE TROPICAL BOHO AFFAIR
Photography by Phan Tien Photography, www.phantien.fr

Words by Phan Tien, of Phan Tien Photography

THE CONCEPT
'Boho-chic' is a concept that conveys the bold personality, liberality, and harmony with nature, perfect for our couple, Heidi and Ruby - two very romantic free spirits. There are no color rules for the Boho style, it's simply a harmonious combination of the couple's favorite color tones. We went for a neutral pastel palette and added a rustic brown color that represents natural plants. Flowers and decorative items are carefully selected, interspersed with striking colors. These color elements are mixed in what seems to be chaotic, but in fact, they are in harmony and bring a strange brilliance.

THE LOCATION
Hoi An, Vietnam, where the shoot takes place, is an ancient city that combines the quintessence of Vietnamese beauty, culture, and history. The local elements are also details that accentuate the creative space: a kayak ride under the sun, a palmed tree-lined ceremony space, and exquisitely crafted products. Our intention is to immerse the shoot in timeless, rustic, and idyllic local beauties.

THE VENUE
An open-air outdoor space is what we had in mind for a Boho wedding setting. Among countless beautiful venues in Hoi An, Vietnam, Anicca Villa, carrying the charming and classic local beauty, is the destination of our choice. Anicca Villa parks on the riverside in the heart of an old town offering a relaxing, intimate space full of sunlight. The stone-paved swimming pool and a tropical garden create a landscape in harmony with nature.

THE WEDDING DRESSES

We aimed to design the wedding dresses to complement each other though still have their own signature. Both gowns are tulle dresses that have a smooth shape with loose length styled with bold nomadic imprints. Additionally, each gown is inspired based on the bride's personality.

Heidi's dress expresses her eccentricity and sweetness while Ruby's transparent gown is both edgy yet gentle.

THE STYLING

For this styled shoot, we wanted to create unique effects by using maximum local elements added with a modernistic sense. The sound of chisels and cuts are a familiar and indispensable part of Hoi An where many traditional craft villages were formed, developed and maintained for hundreds of years. This is why it is an interesting point to bring in typical local products when organizing an intimate destination wedding. Utilizing exquisite crafts to help the couple and their guests get an insight into the destination's culture and, in some way, can understand the traditional values of the destination. We believe that will surely make the wedding more memorable and meaningful.

Bohemian style has long been no stranger to the masses and to make our shoot unique, we decided to combine the modern and traditional by using products crafted by local artists with a contemporary touch. All decorations are designed in a monochromatic palette. Marble banquet table with exquisitely designed wooden frame, minimalist neutral white cloth table runner, dusty pink and orange flower arrangement, and above, rattan lanterns drape over with warm golden light.

THE KAYAK RIDE

An early kayak ride down a river in Hoi An, watching the day begins with a panoramic view of the horizon- a perfect start for a big day. On the way back, they paddle through a coco-palm island of hundreds of hectares.

What might have just been a small trip, it was a trip is filled with precious moments that everybody treasures. There's a certain calmness about a boat ride through the rivers while the shorelines bustle.

THE CEREMONY SPACE

An adorable and passionate wedding ceremony in the midst of green nature with palm trees swaying to the music of love. Along with that, neutral tone flowers dotted with magical mist and beige candles created a divine and spiritual scene for the dreamers. Floating above is a handcrafted rattan crane- a symbol of elegance, escapism and longevity in Vietnamese culture.

THE STATIONERY

The cloth wedding sign surrounded by tropical plants had a small piece of the "Moon River" lyrics in handwriting, which is the best song to reflect the couple's love story. Following the concept, sketches of village trees and the Anicca Villa are added to the invitation suite for a local touch; all are wrapped in a sedge envelope.

THE WEDDING CAKE

The incredibly eye-pleasing marble cube cake placed on an antique pedestal made of tuynel and slate, with flowers and candles all around creates a balance between modern sophistication and antiquity.

Calligraphy Letter And Soul | **Celebrant** Wedding Celebrant Vietnam
Concept & Styling A Passionate Journey Workshop by Phan Tien Photography | **Florist** Amoa Flower Studio | **Gowns** Hacchic Couture
Make-up Thịnh Nguyễn | **Planner** Meraki Wedding Planner
Photography Phan Tien Photography | **Stationery** Flocat Creation
Venue An Villa | **Videographer** Kiba Wedding | **Workshop Coordinator** Hands & Heart Wedding

KNOWS NO BOUNDARIES,

AND NEITHER SHOULD YOUR RINGS.

EXTRAORDINARY JEWELLERY FOR UNCOMMON PEOPLE

WWW.DEBRAFALLOWFIELD.COM

 debrafallowfieldjeweller

A SPECIAL THANKS

Dancing With Her couldn't exist without an incredible network of humans from around the globe who support the publication. Whether you follow along on social media, have picked up a copy of this magazine at a local store or you've found us on the world wide web, we are so grateful that you are here.

This list isn't exhaustive, but it is those who directly contributed to bringing this tenth volume of Dancing With Her magazine to life- it really couldn't be without them.

FOX & KIN
www.foxandkin.com

SHANE SHEPHERD
www.shaneshepherd.com

KIRA MCGRIGG PHOTO
www.kiramcgriggphoto.com

JACQIE Q PHOTOGRAPHY
www.jacqieq.com

JENNIFER MOHER
www.jennifermoher.com

LORENA LEON
www.lorenaleon.com

DEWITT FOR LOVE
www.dewittforlove.com

FOX & TWIG
www.foxandtwig.com

MARI SABRA PHOTOGRAPHY
www.marisabraphotography.com

SILK & THORN
www.silkandthorn.com

JENNIFER SEE STUDIOS
www.jenniferseestudios.com

KRISTYN TAULANE PHOTOGRAPHY
www.kristyntaulane.com

SARAH MCCLURE PHOTO
www.sarahmcclurephoto.com

DANI KNIGHT & CO
www.dkandcophotography.com

AMORVINCITOMNIA
www.ritafoldi.com

PHAN TIEN PHOTOGRAPHY
www.phantien.fr

Dancing With Her

THE DIRECTORY

The Tailory New York, The Hello Bureau, Eve Rox Photography, James White Photography

A CURATED COLLECTION OF INCLUSIVE WEDDING VENDORS FROM AROUND THE WORLD

www.dancingwithher.com/directory

THE LIST

SOME OF THE VERY BEST WEDDING VENDORS

AUSTRALIA | USA | THE WORLD

JACKSON GRANT WEDDINGS
Photography

The only time I'm in the way is when the Nutbush comes on. I snap, I film, and I'm here for a good time, not a long time. Car, boat, plane? Seeya round like a rissole. Anywhere interstate or overseas is fine by me, just feed us some grub would ya?

www.jacksongrantweddings.com | @jacksongrantweddings

CELEBRATE WITH HAILEY
Celebrant

Completely personalised, engaging and heartfelt ceremonies delivered with a touch of humour and zero waffle. You're able to relax and enjoy the whole process knowing you will be guided through it all with calm and ease. The ceremony we create together will truly reflect your individuality and love.

www.celebratewithhailey.com.au | @celebratewithhailey

CUSTOM CELEBRATIONS BY DEE
Celebrant

I'm Dee. A gay, fun, modern, relaxed Marriage Celebrant based in Melbourne. Whatever size or style wedding you are planning, your ceremony sets the tone for your celebration. It's also a chance to stand still, be with the one you love, and share your story and commitment with your family and friends.

www.customcelebrations.com.au | @customcelebrations_by_dee

ONE MORE SONG DJS
Entertainment

No more Nutbush! We're wedding DJs Eddy and Aleks. We love great music, awesome parties and becoming besties with our clients. We are not an agency- the person managing your booking will be the same person smashing it behind the decks at your wedding!

www.onemoresong.com.au | @onemoresongdjs

AUSTRALIA

THE FOX AND THE BEAR
Photography

From the messy chaos of morning prep, to the teary G&T fueled boozy hugs on the dance floor- if you're planning a stress-free day and you aren't afraid to kick off your shoes and enjoy the party, then we'll make a bloody great match! We're based in Brisbane, Queensland, but we happily travel Australia wide.

www.itsfoxandbear.com | @itsfoxandbear

MONTY KING
Celebrant

Your marriage ceremony shouldn't be a chore that your favourite people have to endure, just to get to the good stuff. An epic day that no one will ever forget. A ceremony filled with laughs and tears, cheers and good times. I want to tell your peeps how you met, where you're at and what's coming next.

www.montyking.com | @montykingcelebrant

THE NAKED FLORIST
Florist

Wild, organic and inspired by nature. The Naked Florist honours nature in it's purest form by taking it's seasonal standouts and arranging into your hands, your day and your memories.

www.thenakedflorist.com.au | @thenakedfloristau

BAKER BOYS BAND
Live Music & Band

A live band elevates any event and adds energy and personality to your special day. The Baker Boys are true professionals who are sure to bring the roaring party you've always dreamed of. As your music specialists, we will make sure every aspect of the music on your big day is covered.

www.bakerboysband.com.au | @bakerboysband

THE HOUSE OF BRETÓN
Attire

Lei Bretón, queer designer, makes affirming wedding suits and dresses for queer folx and the people who love them. Our studio stands up for the right of Trans, Non-binary, disabled and neurodivergent people.

www.thehouseofbreton.com | @thehouseofbreton

TODD DANFORTH PHOTOGRAPHY
Photography

A partnership in life and business, Todd and Adam are a Los Angeles-based photography duo dedicated to the art of visual storytelling. They specialize in capturing love stories for the LGBTQ+ community with intention and lyrical artistry, crafting an inclusive experience for all couples.

www.toddjdanforth.com | @toddthephotographer

LENSY MICHELLE PHOTOGRAPHY
Photography

Lindsey ("Lensy") Michelle is a queer, Boston-based photographer that encourages her couples to do exactly what they want for their wedding day! Her style is a mix of candid and directed coverage that seeks to amplify and celebrate what makes each couple unique.

www.lensymichelle.com | @lensymichelle

AIMLEE PHOTOGRAPHY
Photography

Hi, I'm Amy! I am an elopement photographer for the unconventional. I obsess over couples in love and capturing them in their element. I fell in love with photography because of the ability to freeze a moment in time without taking away from it. I love create timeless images that feel like tangible memories.

www.aimleephotography.com | @aimlee

USA

AIDE-MÉMOIRE
Jewelry

Aide-mémoire Jewelry is an inclusive, queer woman-owned business in Seattle, founded by designer, Aran Galligan, that focuses on handmade, Eco-friendly, and conflict-free everyday fine jewelry, wedding and engagement rings. Their mission is to create future heirlooms in a socially and environmentally responsible way.

www.a-m.shop | @aidememoirejewelry

EVE ROX PHOTOGRAPHY
Photography

I'm an explorer and lover of everything by nature. I'm extremely passionate about things I do- it's in my blood. I love bold and golden colors in my photos with a touch of moody vibes. I'm more of a go with the flow kind of gal and try to document your day as it unfolds without so much equipment around me to interrupt your flow.

www.everoxphotography.com | @everoxphotography

TINY HOUSE PHOTO
Photography

Tiny House Photo is a documentary wedding photographer based in South Florida but ready to travel. Mostly unposed, always fun and not just inclusive, we're family. What will your love story look like?

www.tinyhousephoto.com | @tinyhousephoto

GOOD SEED FLORAL
Florist

Good Seed Floral is an all-inclusive wedding floral design company based in Oregon and Texas. They specialize in organic, natural designs that let the flowers do the talking and are obsessed with finding the perfect mix between wild and romantic.

www.goodseedfloral.co | @goodseedfloral

SHELBY ELLIS PHOTOGRAPHY
Photography- UK & Worldwide

Natural light, documentary, story-telling photographer available to capture weddings and elopements in the UK and Worldwide. If you're a couple who are madly in love and value beautiful imagery, I want to work with you!

www.shelbyellis.co.uk | @shelbyellisphotography

CODY CALLIGRAPHY & DESIGN
Stationery & Calligraphy- Canada

Fine art stationery with a modern flair, for all couples. Proudly celebrating LGBTQ+ love, and all things paper and ink.

www.codycalligraphy.com | @codycalligraphy

LORD VIOLET
Jewelry- Canada & Worldwide

Lord Violet is a subversive, yet femme jewelry line influenced by alternative subculture. Brass is paired with recycled materials to create designs that are luxurious, yet Eco-responsible. Handcrafted by queer, independent Canadian designer, Nicola Inman.

www.lordviolet.ca | @lord_violet

WILD HEARTS PHOTOGRAPHY
Photography- UK

Creative and documentary photographer based in North East England, documenting love stories and life stories just as they are.

www.wildheartsphotography.co.uk | @wildheartsphoto

AROUND THE WORLD

NATALIE YUNG PHOTOGRAPH
Photography - Canada

Natalie truly believes love comes in all shapes and sizes. Telling authentic love stories for the intimate and adventurous couples. To me, every wedding I have the honour of shooting, is more than a formal event; it is life, unity, and joy all unfolding before our eyes. I aim to tell your love story the way you want to remember it.

www.natalieyung.com | @natalieyungphoto

JENNIFER MOHER PHOTOGRAPHY
Photography- Canada

I am a documenter of the essence of souls. I believe there is something insanely special inside of all of us and I feel compelled to find that and showcase it in each human and every couple I photograph. I photograph portraits, weddings and elopements. In my spare time, you will find me binging Buffy the Vampire Slayer, zombie movies or singing karaoke. I am thrilled to create art with you.

www.jennifermoher.com | @jennifermoher

KATIE NELSON PHOTOGRAPHY
Photography- Canada

I create fun, colorful, personality-filled wedding stationery for cool modern couples. I'm all about getting to know you as a couple and bringing your wedding-day vision to life on paper. Your wedding day should be all about what you want, not anyone else, and I love hearing your plans, the more unique, the better.

www.katienelsonphotography.com | @katienelson.photography

MARÍA LORIAN
Celebrant- Spain

This is my way of making the world a little better, telling stories of people who love each other without fear, despite the stones in the way. Humans who love each other well, with a healthy and respectful love, and who infect everyone with this love. Because the more we love, the less room there is for violence and fear.

www.marialorian.com | @lorian.maria

ISAIAH + TAYLOR

Los Angeles Wedding Photographers

IsaiahAndTaylor.com

www.ingramcontent.com/pod-product-compliance
Lightning Source LLC
Chambersburg PA
CBHW041123020526
44107CB00088B/2996